THE
GREATEST
BATTLE

THE GREATEST BATTLE

CHRISTY WALL

LUMINARE PRESS

WWW.LUMINAREPRESS.COM

Luminare Press
442 Charnelton St.
Eugene, OR 97401
www.luminarepress.com

LCCN: 2022911964
ISBN: 979-8-88679-013-9

Dedicated to my family, who through their deep faith, patience, ever-constant love, and joy helped me to become the mother and woman I am today. Thank you to my husband who encourages me in all things good, true, and beautiful, and without whom I would be lost.

A special note to the many amazing friends who have walked this journey with me, encouraged me, inspired me, made me laugh, let me cry, and generally made this world a better place: I'm sorry you are not named in this book. If I wrote every name, it would fill pages. I have been blessed to know so many good people. But, for the sake of the story and to respect others' privacy, I have left all names out. If you look closely, your stories are here, in these pages. Your love is stamped upon my heart, and you are never forgotten.

Contents

BATTLE CALL

The soldiers come.
Each in response to his call.
The strong, the weak.
Standing fierce. Standing tall.

The armor jingles
Bright flashes in the sun.
As others hurry in
before the day is done.

Tension thick,
Battle fills the air.
Warriors on their knees
In humble prayer.

And I? I stamp and pace
Against the dark.
Like a restless steed of war.
Here to serve and do my part.

Battle Maiden
Bright as the sun.
With your grace,
The battle is won.

—CHRISTY WALL

CHAPTER 1

The Flame Ignites

MOMENT IN TIME

It was a day like any other day, the Saturday after Thanksgiving. The sun was streaming in through the windows, while the house lay quiet and clean from the holidays. There was an illusion of safety and comfort as though no danger could penetrate the serenity of the moment.

The phone rings, a jarring imposition into the silence.

It is the call every parent dreads. The call that changes every moment hereafter. It is the call that freezes time and from which you never return the same.

"Mrs. Wall. I am so sorry to call you. There has been an accident. Franz is hurt." I hear tears. "I am so sorry to be the one to tell you this. We were skiing and he went off a ski jump. He shouldn't have gotten hurt. Maybe a broken arm. But. I don't know how to tell you this. I think he is paralyzed."

The room is spinning. I am lost and without thought. I grab a handful of items and begin the four-hour drive to the hospital. As I am driving, the cell phone rings.

It is the nurse. "Franz has been injured very badly. He is paralyzed and cannot move from the chest down. He cannot use his hands. He is about to go into surgery. Do you want to talk to him?"

I hear Franz's voice, "Mom."

Oh, my son! My son! My heart splits open. What do I say? What is the single most important message to give him before he goes into surgery, where I may lose him forever? In that moment in time, I think only two things. The most important and necessary things he needs to know. The muscle memory of so many crosses, so many prayers, so many trials, and so many blessings. God has prepared me for this exact moment in time, and I am filled with conviction and faith.

"Franz! Franz, I am driving as fast as I can to be with you." There is a desperate pause because it may be the last time.... "I love you."

"I love you Mom....I think I'm paralyzed."

His simple words almost stop my heart, and I force myself to breathe. There is only one more thing to say, and I must say it now, in case I have no second chance. I speak firmly, forcefully, willing him to hear my words with every fiber of his being.

"Franz, listen to me! God has given this to you for your salvation and the salvation of souls."

"I know, Mom." He says with absolute clarity and conviction. "And that is the most important thing.

"Goodbye Mom. I love you."

That moment in time stands frozen in my psyche. A moment I will never forget. Like a painting; before the arrow strikes, before the horse's hoof falls, before the shadows darken and the light extinguished. It is the moment that changes everything.

But herein lies the truth. The great truth. Each of us is a masterpiece created by He Who Loves. We are like a beautiful painting that has taken years of study and work for its creation. And perhaps even more years for its greatness to be appreciated. The gift of such faith, given to both myself and my son, was the culmination of many brushstrokes, divinely and beautifully painted upon our souls.

It is a powerful reflection to see the creation of faith within our own souls and the ones we love. I hope that my story helps you to see the story within your own lives. I hope that you look back and see how our God is a faithful God and has been with you all your life, slowly drawing you close to His heart. For our God is a loving God, whose love transcends all of time. He is the Great Lover, the Great Heart who calls us each so that we can be with Him in paradise.

This is the story of a young girl growing up in an average town, living an average life. A young girl whom God had the graciousness to see not as small and plain but as a great canvas waiting for his brushstrokes of color and passion. This is the story of a young girl who was carefully and lovingly prepared for battle, the greatest battle of all, the battle for the salvation of souls.

THE CANVAS

I grew up in a quiet town just outside of Los Angeles. We had little crime and life was quiet. My mother stayed home while my father went to work. I had two brothers and two sisters. It was a town washed clean of color. By law, everything was painted tan. Even poor International House of Pancakes with the iconic blue roof had to comply with the awful blanketing of pale brown. My mother even had a brown car. It seemed as though nothing important could ever happen in this quiet, unassuming town, lost in bland tepidity.

My memories of this time are few. They are languid and comfortable. There was little to pierce the soul with attention. For in comfort, our souls are quiet. There is no restlessness and longing. It is only in the discomfort of life that we look outside ourselves for something more; for understanding and solace. *Our hearts were meant to rest in thee, oh Lord.* But instead, we are lost in a garden we did not choose.

I went to a Catholic school where they taught mindless rules and hippy Jesus. I had absolutely no reason to embrace what was presented as a meaningless faith. Even worse, the pictures of Jesus were ugly and printed with no detail and by a machine. Not even a single brushstroke betraying the passion of an artist. There was nothing to inflame the heart and soul with longing or passion. There was nothing to give a small child a sense of urgency of faith or desire to save souls. Our town was not only safe from crime but ignorantly and insufferably safe from sin as well.

And yet, at the age of five, I remember sitting down at a little Playskool table with my three-year-old sister. We would invite the neighbor girls and have "God talks." What I possibly could have said as an advocate of God, I cannot imagine. But there you have it. A hot fire burned within my heart. Not something that was lit, or even fed by me. Purely God's hand on my heart. We took these talks very seriously and they continued for quite some time. When I received my First Communion at seven, I made sure to invite these two dear neighbor girls, so they could also long to be a bride of Christ. When I received that First Communion, I thought

I would die of love. I was quite resigned to this. But, yea, I did not die and simply walked back in line, distracted by the cute boy on the right and trying not to trip over my feet.

My next memory was on a ship. We were going to Monaco to see a princess. I wandered around the ship, agitated at being confined to the limits of the boat, very much feeling like a trapped animal. I suddenly came upon the most magnificent room. It had low, gleaming, warm lights, which shone like flashes of fire on the many bottles. There were rows and rows of bottles, all shapes and sizes with warm, glowing liquids and all the colors of the rainbow. The floor was a deep, burgundy red. It was the most color I had seen in a lifetime. The flame in my heart was fed and burned brighter. Yes, somewhere in the world, there was color and mystery, warmth and passion. My heart took on a longing it could not name.

FRANCE

At the age of nine, I had grown a few more years in my tepid town. I was painfully trying to find my way into society. Our school had a seemingly endless supply of rules: drink water only at this time; bathroom at this time; fifth-grade girls play in this section of the miserable, hot, mindless parking lot; and brown uniforms for all. I bowed my head and obeyed these rules the best I could because that was the only option presented. Unless I wanted detention, which I had plenty of too. I was told to color in mindless "worksheets" and answer stupid questions. The interesting ones were not allowed. I drowned myself in the library because it was the only way to escape the incessant boredom and tediousness. I was laughed at and mocked, but I took this in stride, just an addition to the horror of society. "This is how life is" was all I was told and all I understood.

For my tenth birthday, it was declared that we were going to my grandparents' house. I loved their house. It was musty and full of old books. Books with tales of soldiers and lovers. Farmers who worked the earth and understood the stars. There were beautiful paintings, painted with real paint, women with curved, naked backs, or proper women with arched eyebrows and strange, beautiful clothes. But what I loved most was when Grandma set the table for a fine dinner. And I liked it even more if it was for my very own birthday dinner. Soft candlelight fell on beautiful silver goblets and illuminated glasses made of deep blue glass. Silverware sparkled in the soft light. Plates were laid out with exquisite color and beautiful design, some even intertwined with gold. The plates were so thin and beautiful; I was afraid to use my knife. As she arranged everything, she hummed like a magician weaving the most beautiful tapestry of color and light. I sat in a hidden chair so I could just watch her transform the room. I was in awe that this was for my birthday. I felt so important and grown-up and was certain that, at the age of ten, I was on the brink of womanhood. It was, after all, double digits.

We ate and drank that night; we talked and laughed. My present was a box of chocolate cereal that I was not otherwise allowed, and I thought it was the best birthday I ever had. That night, as I snuggled into sleep, it seemed as though nothing could be more right in the world.

Suddenly, I was shaken awake. I looked up from my warm blankets—it must be in the middle of the night for there was no light on the horizon. My mother said urgently, "Christy, come downstairs. We have to see if you can carry this luggage." I stumbled down the stairs, sleepily. "Luggage? What luggage?" As I followed my mother into the darkness, we came out into the back porch. I was suddenly more awake than I had ever been in my life.

The room was brightly lit and strewn with suitcases, piles of clothing, pots, pans, and kitchenware. It was as if our home had thrown up all over my grandparents' porch. I stood in total disbelief. What was going on?

My father shoved a bright red suitcase in my hands. I nearly toppled with the weight of it for our luggage had no wheels on the bottom. Each piece had to be carried by hand. In his deep, serious voice, my father asked, "Can you carry this? We may have to walk far, so I need to know." Struck with the urgency of the question and seeing the look of worry on my mother's face, I nodded. Unbidden tears came to my eyes, and, embarrassed, I brushed them away.

I crawled to a hidden chair and watched. Now forgotten, I listened to a conversation, which had clearly gone on for quite some time. My mother: "Do you know if we will have anything in the kitchen?"

My father: "I think we will have dishes, but no pots and pans."

"What about clothing, how much do I need to bring? Will we need winter clothing? Bernie, we don't have any winter clothing!"

I continued to listen, my heart pounding with an unknown feeling—absolute pure adrenaline. I finally figured out what was going on. We were moving to France for some time but could only bring one suitcase per person. I was the oldest, so I would carry extra. My brother and sisters were eight, five, and three. Unknown at the time, was my mother's fifth child, resting comfortably in the womb, the size of a blueberry.

The distribution was finally decided and made, with my father carrying the heaviest load. The children were all woken and dressed in multiple layers of clothing. They were too sleepy to ask why, except my sister, Heidi who looked at me with large, luminous eyes. I smiled at her as though to reassure her, but I am not sure my eyes didn't mirror hers exactly. Finally, at dawn, my grandparents drove us to the airport, near their house. With plenty of kisses, hugs, and tears, they dropped us off at the curb. In that moment, the sun suddenly rose above the horizon in a blast of warmth and light. I absolutely felt like a full-grown woman and walked proudly with my bright red suitcase. This lasted about ten minutes until I lost my purse, was scolded by my father, and stepped back as one of the humble child-servants, walking meekly in line.

Heidi walked with me, her eyes as large as saucers, and I encouraged her bravely, though neither of us had the slightest idea what was going on. We didn't even know where France was, much less why we were going there or for how long. We came to understand that my father, a well-respected scientist, had been asked to teach at the University of Paris for a year and share his knowledge and scientific research.

DAILY LIFE IN FRANCE

Heidi and I were now thrust into daily life in France. Our day started out with getting dressed in the dark. We only had a few pieces of clothing, so it was not hard to choose. On the cold days, we wore double, and on the really cold days, we wore everything. This did not seem strange to us, for anything was possible in this strange, new place we were calling home.

Morning sickness quickly overtook my poor mother and so we were responsible for not only cooking and cleaning but all the shopping as well. After school, our mother would give us a shopping list. This was very interesting. We had to walk to the store, find everything on the list and then go to the checkout line. And pray. Every time, we did not know if we had the right amount of money. If we did not, we would get yelled at. It was fifty-fifty odds. Every day, we did this, not knowing how it would turn out. If we did not have the right amount of money, we had the almost impossible job of figuring out how much each thing cost, doing the exchange of money in our heads, and going back through the checkout. This was a chore that brought absolute fear. I would have rather taken a beating than the tongue-lashing from the lady at the checkout. Heidi and I would nearly pee our pants in absolute dread, worried if we had enough money. Eventually, we learned how to count in French, count our French money, read prices, weigh fruit, and judiciously make decisions on what we could or could not buy. However, never, never was the delicious French bread compromised.

Every morning, we arose before dawn and prepared for school. We walked to school, carrying very heavy book bags filled with books we could not read and did not understand. It was a fair way; past the bread store with its warm blissful fragrance, past the stores on the side of the road, up the long, tree-lined walk, with the giant twenty-foot-high stone walls on one side of the street. Those stone walls enclosed our school. And now we turned into two massive, wooden doors, which were clearly built for the giants in my grandparents' storybooks. Across the cobblestones and to our little schoolhouse. There we sat. The teacher, whom we called "Madame," spoke French, which we did not understand. The children spoke either French or their native language, which was not English. We understood nothing. I always had a book from home to read with me. I often hid in my stories while the teacher taught class. However, this was not unnoticed by the teacher. Heidi would watch in trembling fear as Madame, like Captain Ahab, hobbled down the aisle, her wooden leg echoing on the wood floor with an ominous, rhythmic "thud, ka-da thud." Heidi would hiss at me "She's coming." But I did not listen. "Christy," she hissed in panic, "she's coming!" But I did not hear. And now her voice shrill in panic, "Christy! Put down the book!" But I did not listen and suddenly Madame's cane flew upon my desk with a fearful slam, again and again, inches from my face and hands.

We had P.E. with the "professeur" and had to do various exercises. One day we were ushered into the gym and there before us were two poles, each about fifty feet high. They reached to the top of the gymnasium, which was a large stone, fortress-type building. Craning our necks as far as we could see, there on the top, by the rafters, was a bell. Heidi and I looked at each other with terror in our eyes. It could not be. The professeur yelled at the first child in line, shaking his stick. The little boy climbed to the top of the pole and rang the bell, and then scampered down. Heidi and I began to tremble and shake in consuming fear. Child after child struggled to accomplish this feat. Some succeeded and were rewarded with a nod. Those who failed were beaten. One little boy, we guessed he was five, fell from the pole and landed on the mats below. The professeur yanked his pants down and felt to see if there were any broken bones. It seemed the horror could not be any worse, but now we had this, too, to fear. When it came to our turn, each of us to a pole, we looked at each other. I commanded courage to my little sister, and she looked at me, radiating love as if this was our last moment on earth. It truly felt as if it was. The professeur blew his whistle and we began to crawl up the poles. It was good we had so little food to eat and had grown strong dragging our heavy book bags every day, for we were lighter and stronger than we knew. We scampered up the poles, rang the bell, and scampered down just as quickly. We did not fall; we were not humiliated with any fear of broken bones. No. And when no one was looking, we gave each other the most triumphant smile you can imagine. No Olympic medal would have meant as much to us as the glory of surviving that trial.

And then it happened. Early one week, Madame spoke to us. She was saying…She was saying TO TAKE OUT OUR BOOK. Ah yes—the books we had mindlessly been lugging back and forth from home to school in our bag. So, Heidi, and I—Heidi trembling with fear and I with that now common feeling of adrenalin—pulled out our books. "Turn to page___…" Oh my Lord, *we understood what she was saying*! "…and memorize such and such poem. We will do *Dictee* on Friday." Oh, my Lord. Heidi and I grinned ear to ear and the room spun! This was what was going on! We had literally solved one of the greatest mysteries of our time. We ran home excited beyond belief. Until we looked at the poem. It was four single-spaced pages. We had *one week* to memorize this. Fear and adrenaline, our nearly constant companions, sat beside us as Heidi and I began the very serious and solemn process of memorizing that poem. The following Friday when Madame yelled "Dic-tee" we were well-prepared and began, as did all the other students, to write furiously.

REAL BULLIES

At the school, we had a real problem. But first, a little background. The thought at the time was that children would learn French and French culture by immersion. So, all the foreigners were put in a little schoolhouse, which sat in the courtyard, like a little lost beetle, in the middle of a large French girls school, Ecole De Filles. The problem was that, at that time, the French hated foreigners, especially Americans. Every day at recess, they would come tearing out of the halls and doorways with flying hair and screeching voices and chase us. If they caught us, they would set upon us with kicking, slapping, punching, and scratching. This was beyond terrifying. Heidi and I would bolt for the bathrooms. We tried sitting in the stall, but the girls would kick at the stall doors until the locks would break and then rip us off the toilets and throw us around the room. I remember vividly, sitting behind a sink faucet watching the girls try and kick me but I was far enough back that they couldn't get me. We would wait for the bell to ring and all the girls to leave. Whereupon we would arrive late to our class and get a beating for being late. But that beating I was happy to get, for it came in measured doses, not the vicious uncontrolled attacks of the girls.

Every day, Heidi and I came home bruised and cut. My father wanted to get us "steel-toed boots," but we assured him that we could "handle it." And so, we trembled with fear every morning before getting onto the elevator to face our own private battles with the powers of hell.

THE LOUVRE

I could not understand what these girls cared about enough to beat us up every single day. What was the passion that drove them? With this backdrop of violence, fear, adrenaline, and survival, I searched for an understanding of life. During this time, we had many trips to the Louvre. This is perhaps the largest collection of art in the world. I walked through vast halls, built by king after king to store his treasure, in absolute consuming awe. These paintings were two stories high and spoke of battles and victories, lovers, and sins. Gods and goddesses frolicked from pasture to marbled palaces and back again. All a ten-year-old needed to know about love and war was painted as bright and bold as a life she had only dreamed of. My family would leave, find me absent, and go back again, only to move me to the next transfixing painting.

The thing about a painting is that it is just a moment in time. A battle. An embrace. A longing. A view into a pasture of peace and tranquility. We are allowed to see all the details of a moment but do not know what came before or what comes next. Is the battle won, the kiss consumed? Does the warrior fall or carry on to victory? Do the martyrs die in faith? Do the pastures stay lit with soft golden light or does the darkness devour them? We can only gaze and wonder.

I remember paintings of lovers, with arched backs, grasping hands, long intertwined legs, and the most ardent of expressions. I wondered at those looks of desire so strong that the paint or marble could barely contain their fierceness. It was as if they were alive and breathing such passion. My small little self would gaze in wonder, trying to relate to such love. All I knew was the love of receiving our Lord in Communion. I determined that I must receive Him, with the greatest of hearts, with such love and desire. And that furthermore, my embraces with my husband must mirror my love for my God.

The paintings of war were just as marvelous. Thousands of people on a canvas as big as a house. I would stop and look at each single person, so carefully painted. Gaze at their looks of dismay, fear, sorrow, or wrath. Wonder at the horses carrying their soldiers, with wild eyes and arched necks. With striking hooves and flowing mane. Truly this was why God created the horse, to go into battle with his rider and carry him to victory. Often in these pictures with fear, bloodshed, and wrath, the artist painted flowers or trees with captivating delicacy. I am sure it was to show the violence of war upon nature. But it also taught me that, in the midst of strife, one could always find beauty and delicacy.

I gazed in wonder at the beautiful Madonnas holding the baby Jesus and wondered at her thoughts. Gazed at the brilliant angels, sometimes soft and kind, sometimes strong and majestic. Gazed at the saints who withstood martyrdom while looking on the face of Christ.

The bland world of my youth was overcome by such passion and beauty as I could never have imagined. It was here that I came to know God, beauty, war, peace, and heaven. Those paintings were ever-after my tutors for life and love, for courage and beauty, and most especially for my faith. I had seen what I needed to know of life.

That flame, once struggling in a world sucked dry of oxygen, burst into a bright conflagration of love. And this was God writing His love on my heart. He had prepared my heart for such love. As a child, He had left it to starve, and finally, as I was touching the very blushes of womanhood, He stoked the winds of desire and set my heart on fire. A fire that would never again go out.

CHAPTER 2

Arc of Gold

BACK HOME

After almost a year, we returned home so that my mother could have her baby in America. I came back to that starved, emaciated world and would never be the same. I drank from the water fountain when I wanted, went to the bathroom when I wanted, fought the bullies, and challenged every single cultural norm. I could not understand why the girls could not play ball with the boys or why we all had to dress the same. For I had not yet learned the virtue of giving to Caesar what is Caesar's.

When the "popular girls" told me I could be one of them if only I wore my shirt this way instead of that, I just looked at them in confusion. Why did my shirt matter, and furthermore, why did they presume I wanted to be their friend? I just walked away from them. Later they told me I could be their friend if I stopped being friends with a particular girl. This was very upsetting to me, and I began to understand something new. Loyalty. I wondered if those great battles were about loyalty. About principles. What were they fighting about? When I asked questions of the teachers, they tried their best to explain, but so often they came up with "this is the way we do it." And that would never again be enough for me. For I knew very well, that in a land far, far away, they did things nothing like this at all. I began to look for truths worth fighting for, truths I would die for. Truths worth loving. And most importantly, truths that transcended time and place. All that passion I had seen at the Louvre was over a truth and I wondered what that was.

TO FRANCE AGAIN

At fifteen, we returned to France, but only for a short period of time. The "girls" were nowhere to be found, but there was a new enemy and one much worse. There were men in white turbans with white robes. They spoke strange languages and tried to stop us when we walked somewhere in Paris. They looked cruel and it was clear they meant malice. Heidi and I were very afraid of these men, for they always were in large packs, like wolves.

One day, while playing in a courtyard near our home with the other local children, a group of motorcyclists came up. It was a hot day and they had stopped by the drinking fountain. The leader of the group stopped to take a drink. He had no shirt on, cutoff jean shorts, a chain around his waist, and many tattoos on his well-built chest. But what I noticed most was his kind eyes. I went up to him and we began a conversation. We laughed and talked until sunset. The next day, he came around again, this time without his friends. We spent many days together talking and laughing. His name was Christophe and I liked him very much.

One day, Heidi and I were walking to the neighborhood pool. The men in white turbans came up to us and circled us. They began to make strange sounds and calls as they came closer. One of them grabbed my sister. She pulled away and both of us stood terrified beyond belief. Suddenly, we heard the sounds of motorcycles and great war cries. Christophe and his friends had arrived from nowhere, and making great threatening cries, they swung their chains in the air and the men in turbans ran away. I was pleased, happy, and astonished all at the same time. They escorted us to the pool and stayed with us, swimming and playing all day. Then they escorted us home again.

As the summer closed and we were beginning our preparations for returning to California, Christophe asked me if I would kiss him. I had never kissed a boy and was very shy about it. I told him I would think about it. This went on for a few days. Finally, I told him the date of our last day in France and that I would decide by then.

A week before our planned departure, my father announced we were packing *that* day and leaving at four in the morning. I had no way to tell Christophe that we were leaving if he did not come to visit. All day I waited and hoped for him. I decided that I would give him a most simple kiss before I left. But he did not show up. Now I knew there was no chance I would see him. We were leaving at dawn, and he never came to visit before noon.

That night, as the sun set in the great Parisian sky, I thought to myself: "Well, all those saints loved God. I wonder if He cares about me. I am going to ask Him for something silly, but He may understand it is important for me. I am going to ask Him if I can kiss Christophe." All night I made this prayer, "Lord, if you love me and care about me, let me see Christophe one more time."

Just before we left at four in the morning, I heard a whistle. Christophe was outside my window. How could he have known we were leaving in a matter of minutes, never to return again? I ran down the stairs and greeted him with a smile. He said to me, "A French kiss, yes?" I nodded happily. He sweetly kissed me on each cheek and said with the saddest smile, "I love you, dear Christy, I will remember you forever." And then he was gone. Tears fluttered helplessly on my cheeks.

What never left my aching and burning heart was the knowledge that God loved a silly little girl and cared about the flutters of her young heart.

ALL THAT GLITTERS

I stumbled my way into high school, struggling to find meaning in a world that had given up on anything other than the superficial desire for good looks, money, fame, and doing things according to the randomly chosen trendsetters. If only they could see the looks of anguish, desire, anger, and determination as I had seen in those paintings at the Louvre, they would know their lives were hollow and empty. But alas, they had all been raised on ugly Jesus pictures and too many rules.

One thing puzzled me, however. And that was the notion of suffering. In all those pictures I saw suffering.

Longing from the lovers, suffering of the saints. The brutal wounds of war and most of all, the anguish of Christ on the cross. Why was there so much suffering and why did the painters and sculptors all reflect it?

Though this question played in the back of my mind, I had now given into the life of superficial fun, beauty, and liveliness. I did not have any interest in sex, drugs, or drinking, mostly because I saw those things as taking away my control. If "the girls" came back or the men in white turbans, I needed to be ready to fight. But I definitely enjoyed being silly, dressing up, staying shapely, and eating well. All the silly pleasures of a pretty young girl in Southern California.

However, in all this superficiality, my longing for Christ in the Eucharist never left me. It was the only thing that made any sense to me. Christ had died because He loved us, and we could receive Him in the Eucharist. Receiving Him who loved us most, receiving God into our very bodies seemed the greatest act of love that existed. And so, that ever-constant fire in my heart, drew me every day, up early, to Mass. I went to Mass as often as I could, sneaking out of the house early in the morning so I could go before school. My passion and longing directed in a single bold brushstroke of life; adoring Christ in the Eucharist existed in stark contrast to my vain and otherwise meaningless life.

During this time, I was haunted by a continuous dream. I dreamt of Christ suffering abuse and disgrace in the Mass, suffering from bad priests or bad people at the Mass. Marauders coming in to kill a good priest and desecrate the host. This was a time before the internet, and if this was happening in the world, it certainly was not on the news. I cannot tell you what caused these dreams, but they plagued me for four long years. Having no one to talk to about this,

I did not know what to make of these dreams or if there was anything I could do, but it only increased my love of Christ and my desire to be His faithful lover.

At this time, my mother became friends with a young woman. Her husband and a handful of other brave men were starting a school called Thomas Aquinas College. It was built on the revolutionary idea that one should study the great questions in life first—before one studied the individual sciences. Questions like: "What is a man? What is his role in the universe? Is there a greater picture than what we see every day? Why is there suffering on this earth?"

There is a "great conversation" that runs through time, with each philosopher reading what was written and recorded before him and responding with his own thoughts. The reading starts with the pre-Socratics, five hundred years before Christ, goes on through Socrates and Plato, to Aristotle, and on through time past Kant and Hagel. The students have the great privilege of partaking in this conversation through reading the texts and discussing them.

When the couple visited, he would take time to discuss these notions with me. As he spoke, the beautiful battle scenes came to my mind in vibrant color and once again I wondered why man fought. What was worth fighting for, and why would one endure suffering? I enjoyed these conversations very much and began to think about many things.

Looking for something more, I went to a Catholic Bible study, where we could have discussions about the faith. Few were inclined, however, to talk about suffering and the saints.

One night I went on a double date with some of the young adults. I went with a kind and intelligent young man. He brought along his friend and his friend's date, a humble, quiet young lady. I was in high spirits that night and wore a glittery gold, backless dress, which left glitter everywhere I walked. I'm sure I looked ridiculous in a chain restaurant with three modestly dressed companions. My mind was struggling to find intensity and passion, and so I rode society with one foot on either side of Christian zeal and societal glitter.

The young friend was subject to deep bouts of melancholy, and so we talked about suffering. In between happy laughter, flirtations, and engaging stories, I certainly did not give the impression of someone who had spiritual wisdom or a deep understanding of anything. But I *wanted* to understand suffering and felt it was the only true insight into what mattered. And so, grasping at what little insight I had gained, I said to him: "Suffering is good. It brings us closer to God." There was an awkward pause, and the conversation turned back to food and drink, for I knew nothing of what I spoke.

I ran into him many years later, and he told me that my insight into suffering had changed his life forever and then thanked me most sincerely. I was dumbfounded that I could have had any impact in that silly dress and superficial disposition. However, he understood my words, well before I possibly could. What I did not realize was that this tiny flicker of an insight was a prophecy of love that would set my heart on fire. It was a glittering foreshadowing of all that is not seen and heard but that which sustains our very breath: coming to know and love Christ in His very cross.

It was decided that I would visit Thomas Aquinas College for a week to see if I wanted to enroll there. I was assigned to a room of older classmates who would show me around. I found myself in the company of a beautiful trio of young women. They took me in and included me in their evening discussions, fun nights out, and visits to the chapel. I admired them very much, for their beauty, charm, and intelligence. I wanted to be like them. Every fall, while I was in high school, I visited the college. Every year, they took me under their wings and treated me like a younger sister. On one visit, one of those lovely women, Jackie, pulled me aside and showed me a beautiful emerald ring. "Shh," she said with a bright twinkle in her eye, "I am engaged, but no one can know." I was so honored and privileged to be among the few that knew this exciting secret. I was forever linked to her heart after that sweet moment of friendship.

THOMAS AQUINAS COLLEGE

I decided to attend Thomas Aquinas College (TAC) in the fall after graduating from high school. Three things happened within the first few weeks of school. First and foremost, I found the horses and started riding. Secondly, and more importantly, I was given a dream that I will never forget. I was chased by Satan. And he was awful. The most horrifying monster one could ever imagine. I ran to the horses to escape, and he ran with them, easily outpacing them. Then I ran to the strong boys for protection, but their muscles served no purpose and they in turn ran away. I ran to the tutors whom I had come to respect, but their wisdom could not outsmart him. I ran to a priest, but even he held no power over the evil of that creature. And finally, I ran to the church, to the Eucharist. And there, in the presence of God, that wickedness found no entry.

This dream made absolutely clear that all the entrapments of the world were nothing to the presence of God. Nothing else mattered. I set aside my desires for the world and did my best to live only for God. I had no notion of what that would mean, but the truth of this was seared into my very flesh, which still crawled with fear at the memory of the dream.

Following this dream was the third thing that happened. The path that our Lord now gave me to find intimacy with Him. A priest came up to me. He had white hair and a narrow, hollow face. Piercing black eyes, like a crow. He was tall and wore a black robe. He said to me, "Which day do you want?"

"Pardon me? Which day?" He was so serious and intent that I barely dared to look at him, much less mock him or walk away.

"Which day? For confession."

Having gone to confession very seldom, having not been taught about sin and death, I could only blink and wonder why we were talking about days.

"Pick a day," he said, his black eyes boring into my helpless, sanguine, ignorant soul, "and you will go to confession on that day, every week."

Speechless, I could not argue, but picked Wednesday as a random day of the week. Pulling out a little black book and a pen, he said: "OK, Wednesdays at three thirty. Confession and spiritual direction."

And there began my transformation in earnest. This dear and loving priest slowly guided me, answered my questions, encouraged me, and gently rebuffed me until I understood the glory of the Catholic Church.

I came to understand the peril of my superficial ways, the virtue of obedience, and that suffering and penance could bring about the salvation of souls. And most importantly, he encouraged my courtship to a good man, Walter Wall, who was to become my husband.

THE MAGNIFICENT MATRON

At TAC, the students played volleyball on Friday afternoons. As a young freshman, I went to the courts to see what it was about. There was a very aggressive game going on, and I watched in awe. There was one girl, in particular, who was fierce, beautiful, and strong. I was completely enamored with her. She was like a battle maiden in one of my paintings. But then, even more astounding, a young man, with beautiful curly black hair, bright blue eyes, and the face of an angel, reprimanded her and told her to calm down. That anyone dared to catch this woman in flight and tie her to the earth was overwhelming. I found out he was her brother, and thought he must be the most amazing man on earth. I followed him around campus like a helpless puppy and somehow got myself invited to a New Year's party at his house.

He lived about an hour away from us. My parents would never let me drive that far, and so it was a very difficult discussion about how I would go to this party and have a ride home in the early morning hours. I would not take no for an answer, and God was surely on my side. My parents decided to stay at my grandparents' house, which was only ten minutes away, and my father offered to take me to this party and bring me home. Hurray for the parents' sacrifices!

My father drove me to a beautiful neighborhood in Pasadena. As we drove slowly through the tree-lined streets, we both looked in awe at the majestic homes, one after the other, each of which was like a small castle in France. He looked at me, "Who are these people?" Knowing the daughter to be the most beautiful battle maiden I had ever met, and the son to be the strongest angel, I was not surprised. Of course, they would live in a castle.

He dropped me at the front gate and said he would come back at one thirty. Feeling nervous and small, I walked up the brick walk with my coat drawn tightly around my chest and clutching my purse. As I turned the corner of the walk, the house suddenly stood before me, light spilling out from every window and music floating into the trees. There was a broad porch with a heavy wood door standing wide open and filled with laughing people. The lights and sounds of merriment beckoned me and all fear flew from me like those sweet strands of music into the night. As I walked in the house, music and laughter surrounded me like a wonderful aroma.

Inside, I was overcome. The house was full of people. They were laughing, talking, singing, and eating wonderful food. They welcomed me in with great enthusiasm, and I was immediately swept away with their joy. After some time, I found a place on the couch and tried to gather my thoughts. I had never seen such joy, such life, and such love. I felt as if I was in the banquet hall of heaven itself. I looked around and saw that the mansion had seen many years. The ornate woodwork was dinged and scarred. The carpet had seen too many dances, welcomed so many pattering feet on Christmas morning, and celebrated countless New Year's

Eve parties. The ceiling bore the weight of the old mansion with dignified scars and cracks, and the walls carried old but beautiful religious artwork. I realized I was in the dwelling of the rich: rich in love, rich in family, rich in faith.

I looked away from the walls and the merriment and saw across from me a magnificent woman sitting in a high back chair. It was red velvet. She and the chair had also seen many years, but both were regal, warm, and beautiful. She had bright eyes and a smile full of love. I was overcome with admiration for her and the desire to not only be her friend but to learn everything from her. I whispered to the person next to me, "Who is that?"

"Oh, that is Mrs. Grimm. This is her home. She is the mother of seventeen children." Such an incredible woman I had never known. She was the mother of the battle maiden and the angel, and fifteen more! This was her home, these were her children, and I was the most humbled and enamored guest in the room.

This! This! Was my vision. To be the mother of so many children, to be the mother of such life and love. To sit and watch my children and grandchildren love and laugh. There could be no greater goal. The house was only a symbol of her great and beautiful love. I could love like this in a hovel or a mansion for the heart beats stronger and fiercer and transcends the home into a mansion of love.

As a postscript, my sister married the youngest son of this amazing family. At their wedding, my father held a glass of champagne and declared, most famously, "This is a phenomenon!" And truly it was. I have now been dear friends with this great matriarch for over thirty-five years, and she has been my friend and guiding star in all my years as mother and wife.

QUESTIONS TO BE ANSWERED

I had three questions while at TAC that needed to be answered. Was there any difference between men and women, and if so, what was it? Why the Catholic Church? And what was my vocation?

I grew up in the time of the feminist revolution, which declared that men and women were the same. I had my suspicions. I was brought up in a family where the women were respected as strong, intelligent, and capable. But, by this point, I also knew in a very real way that a woman had a terrific power with their dress and their manners. I had used this power to not only secure protection, but to inflame my vanity. In other words, a pair of heels could make all the difference. And let's not forget about a tug of cloth in a strategically well-placed cut of an outfit. France had very well taught the art of subtle suggestion.

While I had only the barest understanding of what it meant to be a woman, I wanted to understand more. So, while studying the greatest minds of all civilization, I searched for answers. I found two principles that changed everything.

The first was from Aristotle, that we are rational animals. And so, belonging first to the animal class, we share many of their traits and instincts. But what makes us different from animals is that we are rational. Or have the potential to be rational. This rationality is a two-edged sword. We can either use our intellect to reinvent things and really go wrong or we can elevate our animal instincts to be better humans. An example of how our instinct and rationality work together is to look at a mama grizzly bear protecting her young. As a mother, she has an intense animal instinct to protect her young. We share that animal instinct. We can override it erroneously and be negligent with the safety of our children, or we can work with our instinct to protect our children. But even further, we can use our intellect to control that instinct. The mama grizzly bear will annihilate anyone or anything between her and her cubs. She destroys without discernment. As humans, we can control that instinct with our intellect and discern how and from whom to protect our children. We don't annihilate other humans, even though our instinct might drive us to consider it.

The second principle was to then look at the animals themselves and see what they could teach us. I was fascinated with how animals ran their families. The male is always the protector. He watches out for danger. He also leads the family to good sources of food and drink. The females raise the young and are generally in charge of the social interaction. With horses, if a young horse does not obey the lead mare, he is sent out of the herd to be dealt with by the stallion. After a beating by the stallion, he runs circles around the herd, licking his lips, asking to be let in. This, in fact, is a pivotal principle in training young horses.

The female animals have a better sense of the particulars and the social interaction. The males have a broader vision for the land and what is necessary to live. The females have very precise control over how the group interact, while the male has the strength to direct and protect the herd. The male and head female communicate with each other what is needed or what is best with an intricate form of body language, both sexes demanding and giving respect to each

other. Their instinct is immune from false pride and errone-
ous principles, and instead recognize the importance of role
and duty. Lion prides and whale pods behave the same way.
This became my working theory, and along the way, while
reading the great masters, this seemed to be confirmed.

Men and women are different, and we need to respect
those differences, rather than mock or bully each other.
However, how we choose to run our own families, depend-
ing on the infinite particulars of the members, has as many
variations as there are couples.

The second question, "Why the Catholic Church?" was
primarily decided along with Peter, "Christ, where else
would I go?" Where else could I receive the sacraments?
Especially, the sacrament of Holy Communion, receiving
Christ, my beloved, in the Eucharist. Where else could I
receive forgiveness for my sins? Still the institution of the
Church and especially the pope remained an obstacle. I
was emphatically and claustrophobically opposed to any
institution or authority. The answer, of course, was the
principle of chaos. Without an organized religion with
a leader, there is theological chaos. Living in the twenty-
first century, I had the privilege of seeing this play out.
King Henry wanted to marry when the church said he
was already married, so he started his own church—the
Church of England. And then Martin Luther, horrified at
his sin, declared that his sins were covered with grace and
the Catholic Church was not needed for his salvation. Fast
forward five hundred years and there are thousands and
thousands of Protestant churches, all of which argue over
every single possible interpretation of faith. After looking
at the history of Catholicism and studying the early doctors
of the church, I did in fact see the wisdom of Christ saying

to Peter, *"And I say also unto thee, that thou art Peter, and upon this rock I will build my church; and the gates of hell shall not prevail against it"* (Matt 16:18).

For the first time, I understood the necessity of obedience, and I nodded my head and submitted. This was exactly as I understood our rationality superseding our instinct. My instinct was to be wild and independent, but my rationality understood the need to obey. Not only do we need to obey the rules of the Church for the sake of order in our souls, we need to obey the rules of the state for the sake of order in our lives. Someone needs to decide which side of the road we drive on! The choice is arbitrary, but the consequence of not obeying can be fatal. While society's rules can be used to suppress our freedom, they can also hold us together and keep us safe. The fine line of discernment between the two takes prudence and prayer. However, as long as we first "give to God what is God's," we can be at peace with "giving to Caesar what is Caesar's" (Mark 12:17).

I did not know how that lesson would come back to me and sear into my very soul.

And finally, every student at TAC took on the most important search, that of their vocation. Their calling from God. Single, married, or religious. This was a constant part of our conversations. After determining that I was Catholic in body, mind, and spirit, and furthermore, armed with a bright understanding of my womanhood, I proceeded to pray and read the lives of saints, hoping to have my vocation revealed to me.

MY VOCATION

One day during my sophomore year, I sat in Mass praying and preparing to receive our Lord in Holy Communion. I had a very clear thought: "I am sending you off to learn your vocation. Be ready." Of course, I had no idea where that thought came from or what it meant and I dismissed it as silly imaginings.

At lunch that day, I saw a notice on the school bulletin board requesting a nanny for the summer in Washington, D.C. I lived in Southern California, not on the East Coast. So, I dismissed it and went on to lunch.

That night, my mother called me. She said, "I was in Mass and had the strong thought that you should go to Washington, D.C., to know your vocation." I almost passed out. I started to mumble and blather and finally found all the words to explain to my mother what I had seen that day. She started to cry. "I thought it was foolish because why would you go across the country for your vocation? I don't want you to leave us." I too started to cry. The whole thing seemed preposterous. I told her, "Look, I'll apply for the job, I think I must, but we shall see what happens."

I applied for the job and received a phone interview. What she asked every applicant, every summer, every time is "What do you enjoy doing with children?" I was the oldest of five children in my family and I had nannied for a few years as well as been a lifeguard and swim teacher. But I did not perceive myself as enjoying the children as much as I enjoyed teaching and organizing them. I would have answered that question badly, had she asked it. But instead, she asked, "What have you done with children?" My answer was frolicking and expansive and I was hired on the spot. I called my mother, and we both cried. It would be the first time anyone had left home, especially for so long and so far.

They sent me a large packet full of maps. I had no idea what I was supposed to do with them, so I threw it in a corner of my room. It did not remotely occur to me that I was expected to memorize the maps in order to know where to go with the children in a busy and confusing metropolis.

I will never forget my first time away from home. Getting on the plane. Alone. Not knowing what it would be like to be picked up by a stranger. Living in a strange home. Not knowing anything about where I was. And, of course, there was no internet. No quick searches for "Catholic Church near me" or even "food near me."

I arrived late in the evening and was picked up by the father of the house. He was very kind and brought me to their home. He showed me my room and told me that his wife would expect me at seven a.m. for instructions. Everyone was asleep, so I said my prayers and went to bed.

"Achoo!" "Achoo!" I began sneezing and could not stop. "There. Achoo. Must be. Achoo! A cat!"

The next morning came early. Jet lag was ugly—seven Eastern time, which was four a.m. Pacific time. I stumbled down the stairs, with red eyes and red nose, and sat at the kitchen table, feeling miserable. A lovely, well-put-together woman sat there, with her morning coffee and a pile of notebooks, papers, and books. This is how the conversation went:

"Good morning. Did you sleep well?"

"Yes."

"I assume you read the package and memorized the map which we sent you."

"Yes."

"Great, we expect this summer to be full of educational activities and mind-stimulating reading."

"Yes. Of course,"

"Also, we hired you because you are a swim teacher, so we hope you can teach the girls to swim."

"Yes. Of course,"

"Excellent. I am off. Dinner ingredients are in the fridge; the recipe is on the counter. I don't suppose you can make cinnamon rolls, can you? The last girl could."

"Uh, no. No cinnamon rolls. Sorry."

"See you tonight, then." And then she was off with a proficient swish.

I sat in my chair for quite some time, wondering what on earth had I done. I was near tears from lack of sleep, homesickness, and being totally overwhelmed. Thank God, I threw the package, with the maps, in my suitcase!

But first things first—we had to vacuum my room and get out the cat hair.

At that moment the girls woke up and we had some breakfast. They were lovely five-year-old twin girls, full of smiles and mischief. I told them, "Our first adventure of the day is to move the bed and vacuum underneath." They thought this would be fun.

We marched upstairs and I grabbed the headboard and told them to grab the footboard and together we would "Pull!"

I rolled over on the carpet with the headboard in my hands. The girls looked at me astonished. "You broke great grandmother's bed!"

At that moment I could either cry or laugh. I chose the latter. And we rolled around laughing until tears stained our sweaty faces.

We moved the bed, and clearly, the carpet underneath had been the cat's domain. It was white with cat hair. Horror. But then triumph. I happily vacuumed underneath the bed, opened the window, and felt a huge sigh of relief. We got some glue, fixed grandma's bed, and put it back. Time for lunch and then we would conceive of another adventure. Or maybe take a nap.

We did indeed have many, many adventures: going to different museums; going swimming—yes, learning how to swim; playing silly games; making up plays; and playing dress-up. Every evening we would happily report our day of adventure with laughter and stories galore. Both parents loved these stories and didn't mind a bit that none of the educational materials were ever to be seen again. I became very good friends with their mother and even after thirty years have passed, we are still friends.

Meanwhile, my mother, who worried for my safety both in body and in soul, found me a young Catholic group where I could attend meetings and have some Catholic friends. Soon after I arrived, I went to a get-together, and as luck would have it, there was a priest offering confession. I went into a room, sat behind a curtain, and confessed my sins. I gave no indication of who I was or why I was there. The priest was quiet for a moment and then said, "Clearly you are here to discern your vocation." I almost passed out.

I began in earnest to pray. Nannying started at eight a.m., so I woke up at five a.m. and walked a mile every morning to Mass and then spent an hour praying afterward, and then walked home. I had a long list of prayers in the evening. I said a ninety-day novena for my husband, whether that be Christ or man. I had no car and few friends, so I spent my spare time praying. I loved being in the church, in the presence of Christ, and so I spent my time happily adoring Him and enjoying His presence. My time in D.C. was like a great three-month novena of prayer, a time of quiet, and few distractions. God knew I needed this time apart in order for Him to bring me close and illumine my heart.

One day in Mass, I sat and compared options. Nun vs. wife—both married to a love—and the spouse of a nun was far more perfect than the spouse of a woman. Nun vs. wife—both could be the mother of children, for as a nun I would be a spiritual mother. Suddenly I had an image of myself in some sort of emotional stress, pounding on the chest of a man. And then I knew—I needed to be married to a man. For I could not pound on the chest of God.

It was settled then. I happily continued my novena for my husband, now confident it was a flesh-and-blood man somewhere on this earth and that he might need my prayers.

That summer, a young man struggled with his faith. Did he really believe? Who was he going to be as a man? By the end of the summer, that very summer, he decided he did in fact believe in Christ, in the holy Catholic Church, and that he would go to Thomas Aquinas College in the fall.

Do not ever doubt the power of prayer.

Our lives were set to collide.

NOT YET

I met Walter Wall that fall of my junior year. I was full of joy and mirth and energy. I was asked to train one of the horses who was as wild as I was. We loved nothing more than to race across campus at full speed, stop, turn on his hindquarters, and race back. The horse felt my energy and I felt his and there were no restrictions to our antics. When I rode, I sang or hollered, as my mood would have it, and I did not care who saw me or what they thought. Walter saw me. He thought I was crazy.

However, Walter came to campus also full of joy and mirth and energy. He engaged in pranks, games, and teasing antics. Finally falling in a serious accident, he broke his hip in multiple breaks, was put on traction for three months, and ended up in a wheelchair. Even confined to a wheelchair, he was full of mirth and pranks. I thought he was crazy.

And so, we avoided each other.

Except one moment in time. I walked past him in a hall, and he asked me "Do you want to go to Mexico?" I stopped. Transfixed.

I had been asked to Mexico by other men, asked to Vegas, and even asked to Europe, and yet I did not hesitate to turn them down. Because of France, I had a basic mistrust of mankind and strange places, which made that answer an easy "no." But in that wild moment in time, I looked in this man's eyes and almost said "yes." He was that compelling, that fierce, that strong. But God's timing is perfect, and the collision was not yet.

GRADUATION

School became increasingly difficult for me. My mind moved somewhere between the practical and the mystical. I could not understand the oblique philosophers and mathematicians. I could not understand why they were talking about what they were talking about. Because if the subject was not in the here or now, or did not explain my paintings, I had no use for it. But I so dearly wanted to graduate.

As finals approached, I asked some very smart friends to tutor me, each in a subject. Those brilliant men, out of the kindness of their hearts, agreed to review the semester with me and explain to me what we had been doing in all those classes.

In my junior year, we studied Isaac Newton. I was having a terrible time memorizing the propositions and understanding what we were doing. My friend explained that Newton was looking for a proof of God, and where else was there to look but the heavens and their movements? Clearly only "God" could move the heavens and the earth. This seemed to explain some of my paintings back in the Louvre, so I was fascinated and now easily learned the math propositions to defend this man's longing for God. In the final, I wrote eloquently, passionately, and with a good understanding of the math. To be honest, this clarity was a gift from God. Because, unbeknownst to me, my math teacher had determined I deserved to fail his class. But my science teacher, after reading my final, went to the math teacher and said—this is all hearsay and rumor, but here you have it—"She showed such an incredible understanding of Newton, clearly she is very bright, you cannot fail her." And so, the math teacher gave me a D-minus-minus. (A double minus as if to say, "You should fail out, but I won't be the one to do it.") And thus it was that I graduated from Thomas Aquinas College by the skin of my teeth. A very great gift from God and my friends who taught me most of what I needed to know.

After graduation, my uncle hired me to help sail a yacht from San Diego to Canada for a client. The boat was a beautiful sixty-four-foot sailing yacht with a fully enclosed pilothouse. Since I knew virtually nothing about sailing, I was hired as the cook. For free. In other words, my uncle needed to move this boat and asked his son, his father, and his very game niece to help move it for free. I couldn't have cared less. I was beyond excited. We went shopping for food beforehand, and as he watched me pick out strange items like a jar of octopus (some idea in my head, I cannot imagine what), he emphatically threw in forty or so TV dinners and some fresh fruit. It was clear to all that I had no idea what I was doing as a cook.

We began our journey with good spirits and lots of excited conversation. Out we went into the blue sea. That night we ate our TV dinners as the sky lit up in a flashy sunset. I was overwhelmed by the beauty of the endless sea and sky.

We slept well, until I was roughly awakened by being tossed out of bed. Hard. Hitting the side of the boat first and then the floor. I got up and went, carefully, to the pilothouse. And gasped. The seas were falling over the top of the boat. I hung on to my seat as my uncle shouted with a wide smile, "Rough seas today!" And down we went, nose first, into the depths of the sea. Everything was a dark, mysterious, and terrifying green, for the whole boat was underwater. My uncle laughed riotously and shouted, "Here we go, if we are lucky the sea will spit us out again!" I looked at him, utterly dumbfounded, as sure enough, we flew to the surface like a bird with its prey. I had no words. I could hear my cousin throwing up in the cabin below me and I didn't know where my grandfather was, but I didn't dare do anything but find a secure seat, with my uncle, and hang on.

This went on for some time. I soon grew accustomed to the rise and fall of the sea and was fascinated by the deep blue-green underwater. I was not afraid because my uncle was not afraid.

I went below once to use the bathroom. As I stepped down the ladder, I saw the most amazing sight. All the objects in the room were flying in the air. The boat was moving so quickly up and down and side to side, that the objects didn't have a chance to rest. It was like a zero-gravity room. An orange flew by my face with shards of glass stuck in it. Books flew through the air, books with gold edges, books that had been loved and read but now were soaking wet with seawater. Food and dishes exchanged places irreverently. The windows all had water in them. And the floor. My God, the floor was underwater!

I ran upstairs to tell my uncle. He gave me the wheel of the boat, gave me some hurried instructions about sailing in the direction of the wave so as not to topple the boat, and shouted something about the bilge. I threw up then and there. My uncle looked me in the eye and assessed my capability. I wasn't going to faint but I sure as hell didn't know how to steer a boat in a storm. He nodded. I was better than a rope tied to the steering wheel.

Don't even ask me what I did. I was consumed with fear. If I did anything right it was my instinct and my guardian angel. I did not topple the boat and within moments the pump was pulling out seawater. No one seemed to ask *why* there was seawater at the bottom of the boat and this seemed to me the most important and frightening question of all.

As the day wore on to night, my uncle looked at me. His eyes were rolling around in his head. He said three things. First, "I'm not a praying man, but you had better pull out those rosary beads and pray." Second, "If the waves break the glass in the pilot house, you will have to tie a mattress on it, so the boat doesn't sink." And third, "If I fall overboard, or anyone falls overboard, do not try and get them. It will sink the boat to turn it in these waves and the person will be dead, anyways, from the cold."

In my fear and shock, I could only think of one thing to say, "How high are the waves?"

"Oh, about forty feet from the middle. Eighty feet from top to bottom."

I nodded solemnly and began to pray in earnest. I could not imagine putting a mattress over anything, much less a broken window in a boat that was diving into the sea every other moment. And even worse, was the thought of having to manage the boat in such crazy seas if my uncle went overboard. I swallowed my fear and prayed my rosary beads.

Those seas in the black of night were like unseen monsters and they threatened to swallow us alive. There is a saying, "I am the storm." I say in response: no, in point of fact, we are not the storm. We are tiny human beings who can easily perish by the storm. We are small creatures, barely able to figure out what is the right thing to do, and if we have, it is even harder to do it. No, we must, like the apostles in the storm, cry out to Him, trusting in His goodness and His help.

And behold, there arose a great storm on the sea, so that the boat was being swamped by the waves; but he was asleep. And they went and woke him, saying, "Save us, Lord; we are perishing." And he said to them, "Why are you afraid, O you of little faith?" Then he rose and rebuked the winds and the sea, and there was a great calm (Matthew 8:23-27).

Finally, the seas subsided and were calm. My grandfather and cousin came out from the cabins below with haggard faces and dark eyes. We watched together, as dawn blushed the darkened sky, and at last, our port could be seen in the distance. With great cries of joy, we staggered into our dock. Our sail was torn to shreds, our engine flooded, and the inside of the boat was full of water and an awful mess. But we disembarked with hearty appetites and plenty of bravado. I had been officially initiated as a seaworthy maiden and I was proud as could be. I dumped the octopuses into the sea, and we all went out to dinner singing like pirates.

CHAPTER 3

Faith and Light

WALTER WALL

That summer my family moved to Pennsylvania. I moved with them. But after a year, I decided to move to Ventura because a young man I was interested in lived in the area. He was going to be a lawyer, so I decided to go to paralegal school. It all made perfect sense. Except that. By the time I worked everything out and managed to move, he had decided to become a priest.

So now I was in Ventura, going to paralegal school with no husband prospects. However, life was not so bad. Ventura is beautiful and even though I was living on pennies, the beach was free and so was the J. Paul Getty Museum, a beautiful collection of art — a sweet reminder of the Louvre. Life was good.

I found a Catholic young adult group and enjoyed the company of good Catholic men and women who were all making their way in the world. I enjoyed the law, and so, inspired by a friend of mine, we signed up to take the Law School Admission Test (LSAT).

One day, I sat with my friends and there was a flurry of excitement. Walter Wall was coming home. Apparently, he was part of this group as well but had spent the summer in Washington, D.C., working for a congressman. Now, he was coming back to Ventura. Everyone loved him, and they were quite excited about his return. They asked me in a flutter of voices. "Do you know Walter?" "Have you met Walter?" "Yes, yes. I have met him." I gestured dismissively. I didn't like him enough to even be his friend. "Y'all just need to settle down."

However, as the time grew near, everyone realized a couple in their group were getting married on the same day Walter was flying in from D.C. He needed a ride home from the airport. Everyone looked around. And then looked at me. As a new member of the group, I was the only one who had not been invited to the wedding. Would I pick up Walter? I looked around desperately but then decided a fun day in Los Angeles would do me good. There was a huge religious store there and I was hoping to pick up some beautiful prints depicting the rosary. This was pre-Amazon days, when a person had to find a physical store. Ancient times.

A friend of ours kept repeating, "I know there is going to be a collision when you meet." Then he would chuckle to himself and repeat the phrase. I found it intensely irritating.

So, I was "it" then. However, a week or so before that pick-up date, my car broke. Heidi and I went to buy a new car. There could not have been two babes more in the woods than us. We knew and understood nothing about buying a car. Thank God the salesman was a good man. I purchased a little Toyota, manual shift, for $6,000, new, off the lot. Only one little problem—I had only driven a manual once and that was across a very forgiving desert where no stops or gear shifts were required.

I slammed into gear and drove like a bat out of hell to Los Angeles. It was a cool day; the sun was shining, and I was feeling very good. I congratulated myself that this was the greatest idea to come out to exciting L.A. Walter or no Walter, for I saw him as a possible liability, I was having a good time.

I got to the airport, made my way through heavy, heavy airport traffic, and stopped at the curb. He came out the doors. We assessed each other. He thought I was my sister because all traces of "crazy" were missing. I thought he didn't look so bad in his tan pants, blue shirt, and navy blazer. No attraction, just no obstruction to attraction.

He got in the car and while we waited for a break in the flow of traffic, I asked him, "So, what's up since TAC?" And he said, "I am going to make a million dollars and then maybe get married."

I nodded and said, "I'm going to be a lawyer." He nodded. Truce.

***

COLLISION

I waited for a break in traffic, found one, and slammed into first gear. A huge bus was in the lane behind me. I stalled out and the bus slammed on its brakes. I ripped it into first gear and literally skidded out in front of the bus. Both Walter and the bus driver exchanged looks. Not sure what that "look" was, but I can guess.

We drove in the California sunshine. The air was cool and fresh, the radio loud, and I was feeling free and good. Walter and I laughed and talked easily in the car.

Finally, we arrived at Cotters, the religious store. I wandered through the store, looking for the pictures I sought. They were images made long ago, paintings of different parts of the rosary. Real paintings, with colors and brushstrokes. Made by artists who cared about our Lady and our Lord. Nothing else would do for my future children. I finally found them. The cost was great, just under $500. However, I had a credit card with a $500 limit. It was given to me by my mom for "emergencies." Clearly, this qualified. Walter thought they were wonderful. I purchased the pictures for my children. They are still in a binder, after more than thirty years, for my children and grandchildren to ponder. May I always be the matron of an old musty home with beautiful books and artwork that sets the imagination on fire.

We went to the beach and had a discussion on homeschooling. Had I been courting Walter, I would have made the proper argument for homeschooling, but I was feeling contrary and argued for the unconventional option of public schools. Walter knew very well the proper Catholic position, and argued it well, but what we did not realize, either of us, was that he was being completely charmed by my willingness to be contrary. I was not being intellectually obstinate or proposing evil ideas, I simply wanted to play with his mind and make him think. As for me, I was intrigued and impressed that he didn't react like so many other young Catholic men. He didn't get mad, run away, or try to control me. He simply laughed and engaged in my argument. Finally, I agreed with him that homeschooling was best. But we had had a proper fun time of it, there in the sand on that sunny California day.

As the sun began its slow, beautiful descent, we agreed it was time to go home. We got in the car and wove through traffic. We were comfortable and happy. I stalled at a red light, and as I was shifting into first, a huge burgundy Cadillac crashed into me. We exchanged numbers, and I went on. My new car now bearing the marks of the very collision our friend had prophesied. Weeks later, the insurance company asked what it would cost for me to settle. I easily told him "$500" and he wrote me a check then and there. And voila! The pictures had been paid for! God providing.

But the damage had been done.

MISSING MILLIONAIRE

I took Walter home, and as he slammed shut the door of the car, he mumbled, "I'm never going to be a millionaire." I laughed and said, "What do you mean?" Though I knew very well what he meant. I just did not dare to think it.

The next day, Walter came to my house with a bunch of the young adult group. I was not feeling well after the accident and was very sore. I lay on the couch while we all visited happily. At one point, Walter asked if I needed anything. Being young and single, my fridge was empty. I told him I was hungry. The other folks in the group rushed in and mentioned that a young lady in the group was having a birthday party. "Was there food?" both Walter and I asked in unison. "Undoubtedly," they both nodded.

We went to the party. I did not know anyone there and was feeling sore and moody. Walter suggested we sit on the floor hidden between the wall and the couch, and there he brought me food. We were there for the whole party, like two little schoolchildren, eating our treats and whispering and laughing together.

Later, the party moved to a bar with dancing on the Ventura Harbor. Walter asked if I wanted to go and, always happy for the sea, I agreed. As we got out of the car and were walking through the parking lot, my shoulder touched his, and such an electrical spark went through me as I had never felt. He put his arm around me, and I wanted to melt into his flesh. Shocked, I quickly moved away. Flashes of paintings went through my mind with such surprising intensity, I pushed them out of my mind. I did not dance with Walter that night and went home with the first set of departures.

Later that week, I received two phone calls. One from Walter's friends telling me he was not eating or sleeping. Confused, I asked why they were calling me. They responded "Could you please go with us to the beach this weekend?" "Ah. Sure. That sounds great."

Second call was from Walter. "Are you doing OK from the accident?" he asked kindly. But something was wrong. I could not hear him. My heart was beating so loudly, his words were dim and far away. I tried not to shout as I said I was fine. "Do you want to come with us to the beach this weekend?" Still, that loud beating, that rushing of blood in my ears. What was this? Why was my heart pounding like an excited cheetah in a sprint? I said I would and got off the phone. This was all very strange.

Meanwhile, I had decided to say a prayer to my grandfather in heaven. He had found a beautiful wife (my mother) for his son. So, perhaps he would find me a husband. I asked him to reveal my husband with a single, wild red rose. In all the flowers I had been given, not one had fulfilled that qualification.

Walter and I and our friends did indeed go to the beach. But first, we met at our friend's house. Walter needed a haircut. Foolishly, I offered to cut it. Having never cut hair before, I had no idea what I was doing. I took a clump of hair to scissors and cut it off. To the scalp. Again. And again. And now Walter sat there, happily, and unsuspecting, looking like a rabid dog. There were a few young fourteen-year-old girls visiting and they were laughing and watching. Without a thought about contamination, I asked them to run home and bring me their razors. They ran home and came back with pink razors stolen from their mother's showers. I shaved the sides of his head bald, leaving a round patch on top. Afterward, God bless that boy, he looked in the mirror, said it was wonderful and then stood up. He went to the wild, red roses growing nearby. I held my breath. He picked...Two roses. I exhaled. Nope. It had to be one. But then, because he is always a kind gentleman, gave one of the roses to the girls. And handed me. A. Single. Wild. Red. Rose.

That was it. Kind of. The heart and mind are not so easily persuaded on matters of love.

We blew up the raft and put it on top of the car, which had no racks. Holding the huge raft while we drove, fighting against the wind, we made it to the beach. Walter found a large stick. And as he pulled the raft with one hand, and held the stick with the other, I thought to myself critically. "Now, honestly Christy, what do you think of this man?" I could only think one thing: "My Mohican warrior."

Walter's millions were now officially lost forever.

COURTSHIP

We all decided to spend Labor Day at a nearby lake. I was still getting strange phone calls from Walter's friends saying he could neither eat nor drink. I was starting to suspect what that was about and wondered what should be done about it.

That day, I sat on an anchored dock in the middle of the lake with a large group of friends. Walter approached in a raft, and as he came, one by one they all dived off and swam away. I thought it was very rude. He came up to me and asked if I wanted a ride in the boat.

We began to talk. Coyly. With caged meanings. Finally, he said abruptly: "Look, I want to marry you. Would you go out with me this weekend? You have until Christmas to decide if you want to marry me."

I have never felt more vulnerable, laying in that boat, in a bathing suit. No heels. No armor. No weapons. Too much. I dived off the boat, swam to shore, and ran about a mile through the grass with no thought of snakes or dangers of any kind. Finally, I sat on a fence. I argued with myself. What was I going to do? Did I have the courage to walk down this path?

Meanwhile, Walter, taken totally by surprise, went to shore and took a walk to think. What could he possibly make out of that reaction? Surely not good. Along the way, he met a bear that seemed to tell him he was like a clumsy old bear. Until the bear became threatened and stood on his hind legs and growled. Frightened, Walter also took courage. He too could roar. And roar he would, for the girl he loved.

I came back without a word. We got in the car and drove home. I was deep in my thoughts and finally decided I would at least date Walter. It was most prudent. But the rushing of my blood and the beating of my heart told me there was much more than prudence on the line.

Walter and I went out that night to dinner and then decided to go to a friend's spa. It was dark and we were the only ones outside. He said to me: "Pick your sword by which you kill me. Dull or sharp. Will you make the kill quick or slow? For I shall die without you."

I said, "Silly man. Why would I be here to kill you." He grew dark and cloudy. He cried in a strong voice "Do not toy with me! Tell me! Will you date me?" I smiled and said the greatest word, "Yes." He enveloped me in a hug such that I could not tell where he began and I ended. Such swallowing of body and soul I had only imagined. But a simple hug it was, and I pushed him away and told him it was time to go home. My heart was so filled with fear and happiness that I could barely think.

We talked on the phone all the time. This was in the days of phones that existed only on cords, and you were charged by minutes. Archaic. We would fall asleep with the phones on our ears, racking up charges and not caring.

One day, Walter said, "Let's go to San Luis Obispo." I agreed, and we merrily planned our trip. We shared our plan with our friend, and he was aghast. "You cannot go to San Luis alone without a chaperone! That is not only a scandal but a grave temptation!" We looked at each other, shocked. We had not thought of that. We had only thought to play by the seaside like two happy children. God, however, always is caring for us. Because our friend's next words were astounding. "Look, my parents have a condo there, why don't we *all* go to San Luis!" Hurray! There was great rejoicing. For our intentions were not impure, we only wanted to be together and enjoy life.

We all went, and it was a wonderful time. On the beach, Walter and I had negotiations. We talked about marriage and how it should be managed. We agreed on everything. Contract read and confirmed. Then sealed and signed by jumping off the pier together and making the long swim back to shore. A leap of faith, a leap of love.

That trip marked the beginning of fall. Time was counting down to Christmas, and I did not know how I could possibly decide something so monumental as marriage. Walter continued to ask me if I knew my answer to the looming question. I did not. I didn't even know if I loved him. I prayed and prayed about this decision.

Finally, in Adoration, I had a clear inspiration: "Christy, my love. You will know my will by looking in Walter's eyes." In that moment I had a clear image of Walter's bright green eyes, filled with such love and endless devotion. It was clear. The thought continued: "You sought my courtship, but I bring you to Walter. Let me give you away to him. You will love me through loving him." I sobbed with joy. My courtship with our Lord had taken a turn I did not expect and brought me great peace and happiness.

I called Walter the next day. I told him I knew my answer. He cried out: "Please, I am in the middle of final exams. What is your answer?"

"Well, you have to ask me to find out."

"OK, just wait. A few days. Until I finish my exams." I smiled just a smidgen at catching him off guard.

We agreed that he would propose the following weekend, right before Thanksgiving. A month earlier than he expected.

THE PROPOSAL

He picked me up from my home early Sunday morning. It was a gorgeous, sunny California day, and we were going to have a picnic at the beach; I wore my prettiest dress and felt full of loveliness and light.

We agreed that we would shop for our lunch. Which turned into looking for a pretty basket to carry our lunch.

At last, we set off. We headed up the coast to a beach. As we drove, I began to panic. I had only known Walter for two months. Had I imagined the conversation in the church? I opened a Bible that Walter had brought for good measure and began to pick out random phrases. None were about marriage. None. Meanwhile, Walter, who was the very reason I had confidence in my acceptance, began acting strange. He pulled over on the side of the road, got out, climbed up on a rock or a fencepost or hill, and yelled at the top of his lungs, "Freeeeeeedom!" He did this over and over. Each time, I became more agitated. I could not figure out what he was doing. Or even expressing. He looked anguished. What did this mean? The Bible wasn't helping, Walter wasn't helping. What were we doing?

In any event, I was hungry. I told Walter to pull over so we could eat. He began to "look for the perfect spot." I finally ordered him to pull over. It was around three and I had not eaten since breakfast. It was fall and the sun was setting, bringing in a harsh cold wind. I asked Walter to borrow a jacket, because in my perfect daydream of a "picnic on the beach proposal," it did not get cold. He had an old industrial jacket and some old Ugg boots. I donned both. We climbed down inhospitable rocks and huddled on the cold damp sand. The wind blew in our bread and cheese. The drinks were cold and not what the body wanted. We ate hurriedly and dejectedly and then got back in the car. We were both glum.

Walter continued to drive north.

As darkness fell and no proposal had been made, I told Walter he'd better head south. I had to go to work the next day. He agreed and we turned around. Still hungry and now miserable, we talked about what we were going to do. I said: "Look, we need to just do this. You need to propose to me so I can give you my answer."

He agreed and said, "Can't you just tell me your answer now."

"Nope, you have to propose first." I was firm on this, yet somehow shocked that he hadn't guessed I wouldn't be doing all this to say "no." But the possibility of "no" was firmly on his mind and he was worried.

He finally said: "I know a beautiful little church in San Luis Obispo. Let's go there."

"Fine," I said. "And then dinner."

It was agreed.

He pulled off the road. It was very dark out and no lights were to be seen. The moon went in and out of the dark clouds in the sky. He finally nodded, "Here it is." We pulled in front of a dark church next to a graveyard. We could see the gravestones in the moonlight.

We walked with trepidation to the door. As Walter pulled on its reluctant hinges, we looked around at the bare trees, dark skies, and luminous moon. The door opened with a groan as we looked into the abandoned church. The moon came through the clouds and lit the room like a yawning cavern. The rafters were filled with cobwebs and parts of the church had crumbled to the ground. Suddenly an owl cried out and flew through a broken window into the moonlight. Just then, the clouds covered the moon, and it was dark. We both shivered and ran to the car. Laughing with fear, we looked at each other wondering the same thing: "Was this an omen? Should we abandon this foolishness and go home?"

No, we had set out upon this mission, and we would carry it through. Walter suggested finding the local parish and asking if the priest would let us in the church. We found the parish near the abandoned church. We knocked on the door. It was probably around eleven at night. Finally, a small door, eye height, slid open. "Yes?" Sleepy. Suspicious. Unkind.

"Sir, I just want to propose to this lady here. Can you let us in the church?"

Door. Slammed. Shut.

We looked at each other. Now we were resolved.

Walter said, "I have one last idea."

Off we went. Walter took me to the San Luis Obispo Mission. They were having a midnight Mass. A youth, electric-guitar Mass. Walter took my hand, "Come with me."

We found a little niche. A place full of candles and saints. It was searing hot in there, and I took off my jacket and stood in my pretty little dress. Walter got on his knees, opened his ring box, presenting the loveliest little ring I could imagine. It was a diamond surrounded by two little sapphires and it sparkled in the candlelight. With tears in his eyes, full of longing, eyes that I recognized, full of devotion, he said: "Dearest Christy, I am lost without you. I cannot live without you. Will you marry me?" I cried out in great joy, "Yes! Yes, I will marry you!" And I brought him to standing and kissed him with such absolute joy.

As we walked hand in hand to dinner, he suddenly got on his knees. People stopped to watch, and he said with a mischievous smile, "Will you marry me?" I paused, pretending to consider, and then said, "Yes." Everyone clapped. We both thought the proposal in the church was too quick and this was a perfect way to extend that moment in time. It was also great fun. So that night we walked through the town and Walter proposed over and over, in all the ways he had considered. And with every bended knee, I said, "Yes." I was forever his.

LEAP OF FAITH

Almost immediately, I called my sister Heidi and told her the good news. Shaking with excitement, we began to discuss wedding dates. May, six months out, was taken by Walter's sister's wedding. Same with June, another sister's wedding. April was Easter and, come to find out, one was not allowed to get married during Lent. The first Saturday before Lent was February 29. Perfect. Nothing like a leap of faith on leap year. Done. I called Walter and informed him of the date, he agreed, and we were off to the races, now having three months to plan a wedding.

It was a simple wedding at the Ventura Mission and then a reception at the Bella Maggiore, a beautiful old Italian hotel and courtyard. There was so much joy and laughter and celebration. Our friend came up to us laughing, "I knew there would be an accident when you guys met." Accident? No. The Keeper of the stars saw this a long time ago. We were blessed.

During our courtship, Walter decided he would take the LSAT and go to law school. He was accepted into two law schools, one in Pennsylvania and one in Washington. My parents lived in Pennsylvania and Walter's brother in Washington. We chose Washington thinking that it would be more of a support to have friends our own age.

We spent a few months in Bakersfield as Walter finished his bachelor's degree in political science, and I worked as a paralegal. I wanted nothing more than that our love would be so intense as to combust and create a new life. At Easter, we were overjoyed to discover I was pregnant. So, even though I was frightfully sick, I was filled with the greatest joy and satisfaction. We only had one car, that little manual car I drove to pick up Walter at the airport. Walter took the car to work and school and I took the public bus to my law office. At the very start of my pregnancy, before I was showing, an old homeless woman got on the bus. She stared at me and said, "You are pregnant with your first son." I was shocked, wondering how she knew I was pregnant. I remembered her words and wondered if she would be right about it being a son. A few months later, the ultrasound confirmed she was right. Maybe she was a witch, maybe she was an angel. Strange things in Bakersfield.

As soon as Walter graduated, we moved to Tacoma, Washington. We had nothing but faith, hope, and a lot of love. We found a lovely little place in the woods of a little island community, Gig Harbor. It was across the Tacoma Narrows Bridge—yes, Galloping Gertie. We settled into our peaceful little life. Walter worked during the day at a bank and went to law school at night. I walked nearly a mile every day to a nearby nursing home and did dishes for a few dollars. It was something to do, and the walk along the woods and the water was lovely. We became friends with a newly married couple next door.

On some nights I went to law school with Walter and sat in the student lounge to watch TV and just be near my love. This became more frequent as my time to deliver the baby drew near. The bridge in winter was very treacherous, and I didn't want to be on the other side of the bridge from Walter if I went into labor. Both the law school and the hospital were across the bridge! One night, as he walked into his final exams, I told him "I think I'm having contractions!" He looked at me, gave me a kiss, and said "Just tell that boy to wait until I finish." And wait he did. Matthew Joseph Wall III was born just a few days before Christmas on December 22, during Walter's winter break.

With great pride, we invited over our neighbors and showed them our new son. They held him and looked at him with such…hope? We hoped too. And then, on New Year's Day, we heard a great rejoicing through the thin walls of the apartment. With no embarrassment, we knocked on their door. "What was going on?" They were laughing and crying with joy as they cried out, "We are pregnant!" We laughed and cried with them. She looked at me softly and said, "When we saw how happy you were to be pregnant and waiting for a son, we decided we wanted children instead of my career." Such great rejoicing in our hearts! We have been friends for all these many years. She went on to have four beautiful children and is an amazing woman and mother.

Our lives took off at a joyful gallop. I promised Matthew that I would bring him a playmate as soon as I could. To our delight, we became pregnant with our second son right before Matthew's first birthday.

The year wound around through winter and summer, and finally Franz was ready to be born. Or so we thought. My water broke on Thursday. Walter arranged to be out of class and work on Friday. It was a warm day in August so, thankfully, we didn't have to worry about the Tacoma Bridge. Our good friends picked up Matthew and he spent the day playing with their son. All was ready. Except Franz. He was not. Once my water broke Thursday morning, I was officially in labor. I labored all day. And all night. And onto Friday. At that point, they found meconium in my water and so we needed Franz to be born. And yet. He would not be born. I was put on Pitocin, and they cranked up the dose every few hours. All day Friday and into the night. I had not eaten since Thursday morning, and I was in screaming pain, with my eyes rolling around in my head. Finally, I asked for pain medication. Before it had even taken effect, Franz finally consented to greeting daylight. He was born on Saturday at 12:01 a.m. The feast of Pope Pontian. So, he was named appropriately Franz Joseph, after the emperor, Pontian Wall.

Somehow, we were able to buy a little house. Oh, the times we had! Painting and fixing up that house, a baby on the hip and a paintbrush in the hand! It sat high on a hill overlooking the Tacoma Dome. You can see it now, painted a bright yellow, a sign of life among the gray of a city buried in clouds. There, our lives were filled with song, dance, sacrifice, and love. Our hearts and hours were full.

<hr>

A SINGLE FLAME

As his law school grew to a close, I became pregnant with my third child. I was raising two boys on my own and was very tired from my pregnancy. I became increasingly exhausted and discouraged. I had no support, no family, and no help. I realized I needed my family and begged Walter to move back to Pennsylvania to be with my parents and family. For Walter's career, this was suicide—we were going across the country from all the law offices that would have hired from the local law school. But my sanity was more important. For four years, the boys had only seen their father for half an hour at dinner. Our family needed to take a breath and reconnect. So, my dear husband packed up his career and belongings and we drove in the middle of winter across the country.

We were very worried about snowstorms and were unsure of how to travel across the country in the middle of winter. Walter knew a professional truck driver from work, and he offered to give us some advice. We spent a delightful evening at his house as he gave us instructions on how to survive if we were snowed in on the road. "Bring blankets," he said. "Plenty of food and water." For this had happened to him. "But the most important thing is to bring a candle. The light and heat from a single flame can mean the difference between life and death."

This imagery lit my soul with a great illumination. If we could only be that single flame in the world, what a difference we could make. In every instance, I tried to bring our Lord's love and joy to the moment. If only we could bring a single soul to our Lord.

We drove off—our next leap of faith to a new beginning. God held his hand over our little U-Haul truck and tow. There were terrible snowstorms everywhere except over our little caravan. We made it to State College, Pennsylvania, on December 24 just in time for Christmas. And on Christmas Day of 1995, the worst storm ever to hit State College arrived with a fury. It snowed for ten days straight and by the time it blew north, we had fifteen feet of snow piled around the house. God brought us safely to our new destination and protected us along the way. We were cozy and happy, embraced with love, family, and a roaring fire to fight off the cold, harsh winter.

CHAPTER 4

Highway to Heaven

✦

ALL THINGS ARE POSSIBLE

When the snow stopped falling that first Christmas, the boys wanted to play outside. Out came the snowsuits and the hats. Then the arguments with rebellious fingers in mittens, and then... "Mama I have to go pee..." Finally, outside we went. It was cold and wet and hard to move in the snowman suits. So back inside. And then...Bored. Restless. "Can we go back outside?" I began to miss California, where we both had grown up.

Walter went to a bar prep class about an hour away in Harrisburg. It was a year of record snow and ice. We prayed him back and forth every day, and on too many days he came home with reports of other cars' grievous accidents and slides into the nearby river. Walter was and is a remarkable driver, and I only recently found out he took a class in emergency vehicle driving, which included driving in dangerous winter conditions. God knew back then and provided Walter the tools he needed.

We waited excitedly for spring. Warm weather, flowers, and best of all, the birth of our first daughter, Katie. Katie arrived peacefully and lovely. With Grandma and Grandpa seeing her right away. It was so wonderful to have my family praying in the waiting room while I delivered my baby and to be at my side soon after to adore and kiss my baby. I glowed in the familial support.

Walter took the Pennsylvania bar exam and when we found out he had passed, there was great rejoicing! He was now a full-fledged lawyer and we were full of hope.

However, we lived in a small town and there was an excess of young lawyers looking for work. The full ramification of changing towns hit us hard. The locals were hiring locals, and no one had room for a lawyer who had gone to law school across the country. Try as we might, there were no jobs, and as the spring weather turned to summer both the loss of income and the humidity began to suffocate us.

We had many fights that summer about what to do. I dreaded leaving the security of my family, but my husband needed a job. We finally agreed that we would go where he was hired. Within a few days, he let me know that he had been hired by a firm in central California. And, "Oh, by the way, I am starting on Monday." The Monday that happened to be coming up in four days. In the interview, he had not mentioned we lived in Pennsylvania for fear it would discourage an offer.

With crying and the saddest of goodbyes, we packed everything into a U-Haul and once again made that trip across the country. A different trip, one filled with sadness but accompanied by a sweet new little girl and a husband who had a job. In three days. And 2,700 miles.

We arrived Sunday night, tired and beleaguered. Monday morning, Walter showed up for work. I spent the day looking for apartments and finally found one that overlooked the mountains and had a miraculously low price. I did not realize it was Section 8 housing or even know what that was. Walter came home to a new home and a new job. And a new fear.

When he came into the law firm on his first day of work, he was shown his office. There on the desk was a contract for only three months of work. He was required to write a legal opinion in one of the most complicated areas of the law. Environmental law. Constantly changing. Rife with politics. All of its laws filled five boxes of three-ring binders. No one wanted to touch it. If, after three months, he had successfully written the opinion, he would be hired in a full-time position as long as he passed the California Bar Exam. After three months, he could be let go, and if he did not pass the California Bar, he would not be hired permanently. And of course, not by any other law firm in California. It was a gamble of everything.

Once again, after a wonderful eight months of family time, it was Daddy at dinner. Walter got up at three every morning to study for the California bar, then go to work and face what seemed like an impossible amount of research. But with God, all things are possible. And hard work. And sacrifice. And love. And patience. Our Lord quietly molding us, teaching us these things. Our love providing the fire of the furnace and His most loving hands sculpting out virtues.

Walter successfully finished the legal opinion and was now recognized and admired as being proficient in such a difficult area of the law. Soon afterward, he took the bar. We waited to see if he had passed. We had gambled everything on that test. If he failed, he would be out of work and we had nowhere to go. Again, we put our faith in God, having done all we could do. It was now up to Him and we were subject to His holy will. With anxious hearts, Walter pulled up the results of the test. Walter passed the California bar! We were overcome with relief and joy. We had gambled and won! The owner of the firm shook Walter's hand and hired him full-time.

Another thing happened. Our law school loans kicked in. The cost of a mortgage. Every month. When we were offered school loans, we were not informed of things like interest. How much our monthly payment would be. How long we would pay—thirty years. How the interest would accrue—after thirty years we would have paid triple the amount we borrowed. And so just as we started to rise, we were crushed to the ground.

We bowed our heads and prayed. We clung to our faith and to our Lord, once again gaining strength from our trust in Him. Making ends meet was a daily prayer that we made to the Lord. And yet, and yet. The love in our home was overwhelming. So much joy, so much laughter, song, and dance. And so, when we found out we were pregnant with our fourth child, there was only rejoicing and laughter. God had blessed us with a new life, and He would find the means to pay for this child.

SALT OF THE EARTH

We lived amongst the poorest of the poor. They were Hispanics who worked in the field, and they were the salt of the earth. I became friends with an older woman and her young daughter, also a single mother, who lived next door to us. We had many talks about motherhood and raising strong children. She had much to teach me, for her strength had been formed through years of battle and struggle. Those paintings in the Louvre came alive in her face as she talked.

My children were as white as one could imagine, with shocking blond hair and pale skin. They loved life and loved to play outside in the sunshine. The other children were dark with sparkling eyes and quick in their movements. I would sit in the sun and happily watch the children play together.

A young single mother, trying to make money to buy milk for her babies, made Christmas wreaths out of a wire coat hanger and yarn. She found an old ornament and strung it on. I happily paid her twenty dollars and proudly displayed it on my door. Every Sunday morning, the police, fire, and ambulance would come for an overdose or domestic crime, and my children would watch the trucks arrive with great interest. Often the grandmother would come out on the deck with me, and we would pray together for the family.

One warm evening, there was a knock on the door. A few of the field workers stood outside our door with large five-gallon containers of strawberries. With gestures and exchange of two languages, we went to the patio below and the whole community sat around eating strawberries. We ate until we could eat no more, laughing and watching the children play. They stumbled through awkward translations so we could understand their stories and we did the same. It was an evening filled with community and goodwill. Culture and languages had evaporated.

At Christmastime, we could not afford a tree and I expressed this privately to my matronly neighbor. The next day a beautiful tree was on our doorstep with a familiar-looking ornament, so much like the one on the yarn and wire wreaths. From her confusing explanation, I had a strong notion it had been stolen, but all I knew for sure was that it was a gift given in humble love. We proudly displayed it in our window, with the humble ornament in a place of pride.

One day, our apartment was spray-painted with gang signs. I asked my neighbor, and she said our apartment had become the object of a gang war. She had a shotgun in her hands. She said to me: "No one will harm you. You are under my protection. I've known these boys since they were babies, and they will not harm me or those whom I protect." And she shot the gun in the air for emphasis. I was too stunned to speak, but oh so glad for her protection.

On Franz's birthday, I planned a party and invited a family from Walter's work. It was the only English-speaking family I knew with small children. When she told me she could not come, I was very sad. I did not know how to tell Franz he was not going to have a party. He was four and very much wanted a party. Inspired by the Gospel of Matthew— "Go out and invite as many as you find"—I went out and invited all the neighborhood children. It didn't matter that we didn't share the same language. Joy is the same in every tongue. We sang Mexican folk songs, played musical chairs, pin the tail on the donkey, and someone even brought a piñata. All the children had so much fun.

I will forever be thankful to that community for welcoming me. This community of Hispanics gave us an example of kindness, loyalty, and community. Our good Lord showed us what it meant to be the salt of the earth. *You are the salt of the earth. But if the salt loses its savor, how can it be made salty again? It is no longer good for anything, except to be thrown out and trampled by men*" (Matthew 5.13). God did not want us to forget.

HEART OF A HERO

One day, the boys wandered off, and while they were safe in the immediate community, we also knew very well that we were in a very bad part of town and the possibility of the boys being stolen was high.

I called Walter and he told me to call the police if I didn't find them in ten minutes. I looked everywhere and asked my neighbors to help as well. Finally, the mother who had made the wreath found them. They were out exploring. They had thrown their little bike over a chain-link fence, and Matthew had crawled over the fence. He urged Franz to crawl over it as well, but being younger, Franz fell and cut his head. They were both sitting on the other side of a high fence, with Franz injured and no idea of what to do. The police arrived and we managed to get both boys and the bike back over the fence and off to the ER for stitches. This was honestly the best outcome we could have had. In a gang-ridden neighborhood, it could have been much, much worse. And so, we sadly realized we needed to move.

God blessed Walter with a raise. We moved to an apartment closer to his work, and it was with sadness and great reflection that we left the community of Hispanic field workers.

We had by now, come to know a wonderful family with nine children. They were older than us and wiser, having experienced much of the many crosses of life. And yet, still, they were filled with joy and a deep Catholic faith. We were very inspired by them and counted ourselves blessed to know them. They welcomed us into their tiny home full of children and so much love. One of their daughters, Mary, became our babysitter and the children loved her.

Now very pregnant with our fourth child, we began to make plans for going to the hospital. However, being in a new town, we were worried about who would watch the children if we had to leave in the middle of the night. Mary was going to come during the day, but she was too far away to come in the middle of the night, if that was when the baby chose to come. We prayed and prayed for a solution.

One evening, the neighbor across the street, whom we had exchanged friendly words with, came to us and said he had a strange dream. He dreamt that we came to his house at two in the morning and asked him to watch the children while we went to the hospital. Though, looking back, he could have had bad intentions, we had a good feeling about him, and we took this as an answer to our prayers. A few days later, I went into labor around three a.m. and Walter knocked on this stranger's door. The man opened his door and said, "Oh, you are late. I've been up waiting for you." He came over and slept on our couch while I delivered our third son and fourth child. Mary came over around eight so he could go to work. Everything was blessed and beautiful. Bernhard Robert Michael Wall was born around eight a.m. with no complications.

We continued to struggle in poverty yet trusting in God as if everything depended on him and working as if everything depended on us. I had my hands full with four little ones. Going to the doctor was a challenge, for I had one in a car seat and three in the hand. I held on to the two youngest and ordered my oldest, Matthew, to never let go. When I arrived at the doctor's office, I was asked, "Do you have help?" Every. Single. Time. And every time I told them the truth. I had no help. But still, those paintings haunted every corner of my mind. Did I or did I not have the passion and strength of the great heroes? I willed those doctors to see the joy those children brought me, help or no help. I would not change a thing.

We were still in desperate need of a better job. So, when Walter was offered a job in Fresno, paying more, with better insurance, there was much rejoicing and praising of God. This job was with the county of Fresno and for the first time in our lives, Walter would have an eight-to-five day. I was overwhelmed with happiness and thanksgiving to a God who is always good.

And so it was, that on a foggy night in January, with my four-month-old baby and three others, I followed Walter driving the U-Haul into the night. For a long, long way, I could only see his red taillights. In the fog, their shape blurred and looked like hearts. I thought with a happy contemplative sigh, "I am, once again, following my hero's heart."

THE PROVING GROUND

The fog we drove through on that January night never lifted. Locals explained to us that it was called "tule fog." A thick fog that lays in the Central Valley of California. We moved in October, and it was five months before we saw the backyard. Cold. Dense. And dark.

We resolved to find our forever home, above the fog. We drew a sixty-mile radius circle around Walter's work and began to look for a permanent home. Every weekend, we took drives around the Fresno area. One weekend, we drove up into the mountains, out of the fog, into beautiful green rolling hills. The sun shone on sparkling streams and granite outcroppings of rock. The beauty took our breath away. From there on out, we drove into the mountains every weekend, looking for a home.

Meanwhile, Walter was offered a very nice job at a big firm on the outskirts of town, as close as one could possibly get to where we wanted to live. Walter happily took the job. We soon found an incredible, big, six-bedroom home, which sat high on a hill surrounded with pastures filled with wildflowers. It was a display model that the building company had decided to sell, and so the price was low. We instantly fell in love with the home. What an incredible place to raise children! Watching my sweet daughter, Katie, dance among the wildflowers filled my heart with an indescribable sense of beauty.

While we waited for escrow to close, Walter and I found a book that inspired us greatly. It was *My Antonia*. It is a beautifully written book, describing a strong woman who made her life in the country. We were very inspired by the last description of the woman:

> "She was a battered woman now, not a lovely girl; but she still had that something which fires the imagination, could still stop one's breath for a moment by a look or gesture that somehow revealed the meaning in

common things. She had only to stand in the orchard, to put her hand on a little crab tree and look up at the apples, to make you feel the goodness of planting and tending and harvesting at last. All the strong things of her heart came out in her body, that had been so tireless in serving generous emotions. It was no wonder that her sons stood tall and straight. She was a rich mine of life, like the founders of early races."

"The founders of early races." This quote dug deep into my soul. I began to contemplate the idea that time was beyond me and beyond the "now," and that I was creating something permanent. On a natural level, I wanted to create a legacy of strong and good children. Those glorious images of battle filled my soul once again. What was I battling for? Something more than what I could bring to this earth? Something spiritual? Something eternal? What, in fact, was the greatest battle of them all?

But this was only the proving ground. A place to prepare us for the next step in our journey. Our sweet Lord had given us the merest glimpse of what He wanted. He whispered to us that our purpose was for something greater than ourselves. Something beautiful and majestic that we could not see. He lit our hearts on fire with a divine purpose that transformed the daily dishes and cleaning of toilets into an act of profound love and prayer.

The new firm expected Walter to complete a specific number of billable hours. This caused Walter to work six days a week and Sunday to catch up. We seldom saw him, and "thank God it's Friday" did not exist because there was still Saturday. My four little ones had a wonderful place to play both in the large house and on the beautiful property, but our family life was deprived of one of the most important elements: the father. The Dad. Daddy.

My brother married an incredible woman, Nicole, and we became close friends. She too was a lonely wife to a husband who worked long hours in a law firm. We consoled ourselves and encouraged each other on many an evening as we made dinner yet again knowing our husbands would not be there to eat it.

This was a time of wonderful, holy reflection. We spent many hours on the phone talking about the virtue of being a good wife, what was important in motherhood, and the purpose of what we were doing on this earth. All these conversations were leading to the same end—what was our purpose as mothers? As saints? As women? What was the great battle we were fighting? The incredible mountains we lived in "lifted mine eyes to the hills" and inspired me toward greater things. What they were, I could not yet see. He was teaching me lessons that I would need later. Letting me practice before the battle.

Soon I became pregnant with my fifth child. A girl. A very strong energetic girl. She banged around in my womb, surely frustrated at the confinement. A few months before she was due, I went into preterm labor and was put on bed rest. It was so difficult having four young children and having to lay down all day. We hired a local girl to shop, clean, and make dinner. I humbly offered up the sacrifice of having *to be* instead of having *to do*.

At the beginning of the year, Walter managed to reserve a few days to go camping with the family. This time off was very special and did not come easily. However, when summer warmed the earth and those few days came near, I was still on bed rest. The campground was far from any hospital. Rather than give up the family vacation, Walter proposed to take the kids camping while I stayed home. Though this broke my heart to stay behind, I knew it was so good for the children to spend time with their father. However, I was worried about being home alone. When Nicole heard this, she so kindly and heroically offered to come to my house to stay with me in case I went into labor. Salt of the earth.

Sure enough, that night after all the kids piled in the car, filled to the brim with camping gear and high spirits, I lay in bed and could feel my daughter pounding on my womb. With dread, I could feel my body start to contract. I woke up Nicole and off we went to the hospital. I was put on very strong drugs for the night and finally my womb settled down. I prayed, "Lord, if you need to take this wild soul now, so that she makes it into your kingdom, then do so." That moment. That prayer. That offering. It was the gift of perspective from the Holy Spirit. What mattered most was heaven, even if death came early. In point of fact, Analise barely made it to full term. And then, while in labor, she refused to be born, almost having to be delivered by C-section. She is my most fierce and strong-willed child and always an inspiration of strength and beauty to me.

Walter and I discussed his crazy work schedule, and though our domestic life was good, not having a father around was not. He began to look for another job. When he found one in Ventura, I was furious. I did not want to leave my beautiful home, the gorgeous rolling hills, the wildflowers, and the forever sky. We had many strong discussions on the matter, but finally, once again, I had to follow my husband.

Our Lord knew. He had prepared my soul. For what was to come next in my journey. The answer to The Question. This was only the proving ground.

RICH SOIL

Walter secured a job in Ventura, and we decided to live in Santa Paula. There was great rejoicing on many a heart as our move became a college reunion. Many of our classmates from Thomas Aquinas College lived in Santa Paula and worked at the college. They quickly came together and found us a home in the center of them all. There was a glorious multitude of large Catholic families living in that little town. Suddenly my children had an abundance of friends! They went in large packs, up and down safe little side streets, riding bikes, skipping in pretty dresses, laughing, and telling tales. The boys were in Boys Scouts with thirty other boys their age. The girls were in Little Flowers with grand tea parties. Library day was a cacophony of young, excited readers. There were young college students who worked as tutors from the college and a bevy of young teenage girls to babysit. We were thrown from the quiet solitude of the country to the exciting vibrancy of a strong, Catholic community.

One of the best parts about being in Santa Paula was that I was only forty-five minutes from my sister, Monica, who was adding to her beautiful family. We got together on many a day, my house filled to the brim with young children and laughter. In the evening, Walter would come home from work, see the home demolished by so many children, and declare it was tacos and margaritas night. We would go to the local Mexican restaurant and lay out our kids in a long row of tables. Walter would sit at the head of the table with a wife on the right and a sister-in-law on the left. It was the happiest table in the house!

I was soon pregnant with my sixth child, a girl as well. But this one was vastly different. She rolled happily within my womb and caused no disruptions. She was due in May. Walter and I had a name planned out for her. But on April 16, I woke up and had the absolute conviction that her name should be Bernadette. Walter and I had alternated picking names, and this was his baby to name. I could not shake the conviction that her name should be Bernadette. When Walter came home, I made a nice dinner, gave him a big kiss, and then sat him down. He grabbed my hands at that moment and said, "Honey, I know we picked a different name, but I think her name should be Bernadette." I was overcome and burst into happy tears! It was not until many years later that we realized April 16 is the Feast of St. Bernadette.

Monica came to my house on Bernadette's due date, and we sat in the sun among the flowers. As the day gently came to a close, I started to have contractions. I drove to the hospital, and sure enough, I was in labor. I called Walter and he came from work. Bernadette was born, sweetly and gently as was her temperament.

I enjoyed the friendship of so many good women, and we enjoyed teas, coffees, dinners out—any excuse to have some fun and talk about our faith and raising children as young Catholics.

I was thrilled to reunite with Jackie, my beautiful friend from those early college years. She had found love before me, married before me, and was now quite a fortress of matriarchy with nine children, all of whom were beautiful like their mother, homeschooled proficiently, and in a magnificent home. I was pleased to see that my admiration of her had been true. Our friendship grew quickly and soon we were back to "girls' nights out," with lots of laughter and encouragement. I eagerly listened to her wisdom and experience and was excited to follow her. She was the best big sister I could have ever asked for.

During this time, we were very happy, and life was good. I wanted to be as far away as I could from suffering. And yet, providentially, I was reading two very intense books. The first was the story of St. Gemma and the second was *The Life of St. Francis*. Both saints suffered great trials in order to be close to Christ. St. Gemma described her suffering as the marriage bed of Christ. Her intimacy with Christ was to join Him on the cross and share in His sufferings. These thoughts were overwhelming and yet absolutely inspiring to me. Walter and I had gone through so many trials and so much fear and pain that I did not want to ask for suffering. I was terrified of more suffering. And yet... And yet... This idea of suffering in order to bring us closer to Christ. This idea that took its birth at the Louvre in the shadow of those gorgeous paintings. This idea that was but a tiny unseen seed while in high school. This idea had been growing silently below the earth, in the quiet of my soul, and now was trying to find the light of day. But I was afraid. So, I asked our Lord what to do. He showed me my heart, that it was good and true. I was inspired with this prayer: "Lord, help me to love you more and more each day." This prayer I could say with the greatest of strength and conviction. And so, I did. In Mass. In the early morning hours of Adoration. While cleaning up spills and changing diapers. I united every moment of every day into an act of love for Christ. It was what I could do. It was the battle I could fight. And the soil became rich with little daily offerings of love and sacrifice.

***

JACKIE

When I became pregnant with my seventh child, a little girl, we were happy to ask Jackie and her husband to be the godparents. As my pregnancy came to its end, I was glad for her support as we faced the birth. Margaret—Walter had named her after his English side—was being difficult. She would drop and then…not be dropped. We tried everything to get her to drop into the birth canal, but she would have none of it. I told Walter one night, "I swear this girl is bracing against the contractions and fighting being born."

As it turns out…I was right. My water broke and still no labor. I was put on Pitocin and finally the baby started to drop. The nurse checked my dilation and then cried out. "Oh! She just grabbed my hand!" I didn't know whether to smile or not. The nurse didn't look happy. She said to me, "We have to do an emergency C-section, or her shoulder will break coming out and she could permanently lose the use of her arm."

And so, I was laid out like Christ on the cross. Arms stretched out, drugged, and wheeled into surgery knowing I was to be cut open. I was beyond traumatized.

When I awoke, in searing pain and massive mental confusion, I was presented with a beautiful, sweet baby. The crucifixion resulted in the most beautiful life. Margaret was a sweet, amazing baby, easily happy, nursed wonderfully, and made all her brothers and sisters laugh. I had an incredible community of girls coming to my house every day to help and I healed quickly. God had seared into my soul that surrender and pain can lead to the greatest of joys.

I did not know I would soon watch my "big sister" endure the greatest pain and permanent surrender while we could only hope for the greatest joy.

I became pregnant with my eighth child at the same time Jackie was pregnant with her tenth child. I was so happy to share our pregnancies together.

Then she got sick. We thought it was a bad cold, but she did not get better. No one knew what was wrong. She got sicker and sicker. We watched in horror as she got terribly thin, her hair fell out, and she was making strange decisions. And still no one knew what was wrong. She gave birth to her baby, a beautiful son. But she did not recover. Our hearts broke every day we were with her. She loved her children and was in great sorrow over not being able to take care of them. Her worry and anguish were devastating to watch. We all came together and took over as many things as we could. A community adopting her children and her home.

At long last, the doctors came back with a positive test. She had Valley fever. In her brain. One percent of people get Valley fever. One percent of them get it in the blood. One percent of those get it in the brain cells. Where it is fatal. The odds were so slim that we could only presume God had given her this disease. The random chance of it was impossible, and only one other person, ever, in the history of the recorded medical world, had Valley fever in the brain. That person died. It was all the doctors had to say.

Soon, she was taken to the hospital and put on IVs and oxygen. Her baby was not even one. We organized visits so she was never alone. We all. Each of us. Watched her die. Held her hand as she struggled for breath. Because it took weeks. And finally, she could not talk and could only wink with one eye or the other. She remained strong in faith and great in love until the very end.

On a night visit, Jackie asked Walter to read her night prayers. The Liturgy of the Hours, the great readings that all priests say five times a day. All in unison. This was what he read. With his voice choking in his throat, for she was living out this terrible agony.

"Lord, listen to my prayer: turn your ear to my appeal. The enemy pursues my soul; he has crushed my life to the ground; he has made me dwell in darkness like the dead, long forgotten. Therefore, my spirit fails; my heart is numb within me. I remember the days that are past: I ponder all your works. I muse on what your hand has wrought and to you I stretch out my hands. Like a parched land my soul thirsts for you. Lord, make haste and answer; for my spirit fails within me. Do not hide your face lest I become like those in the grave." (Psalm 143:1-11)

And finally, our dear Jackie died. I was overcome. I could not understand how God could allow her death. Not with so many young children in her care. Not the beautiful, strong, vivacious Jackie, so full of life and laughter. I was gutted and empty.

We went to her funeral and could not believe that the woman in the coffin, in all her familiar clothing, her hair done just so, was dead. It devastated our community. She died strong in the faith, and we were certain we had all known a saint.

Life went on, however, and soon I was preparing for my son to be born. This was technically my turn to name a child, but Walter's mom, who had never asked for anything our entire married life, asked me to name our son after his dad and his dad's Uncle Walter who had just died. Finally, I promised her that if he was born looking like an Englishman, I would do so. Every single one of my children was born looking like an Austrian with strong compact muscles and dense bodies.

Finally, William was born. He had pale skin with long thin arms and legs. He looked more like an Englishman than any of my other children! I laughed out loud and said, "Well, hello Walter William Wall the Third!"

A few months later, I sat by the pool, nursing my baby and watching my children swim. My mind was calm and warmed by the sun. In that moment of quiet, I had a flash of realization. Jackie had shown me a ring, and then while apart from me, had gotten married. I knew she was married but did not see the ceremony. Then I saw her again after she had many children. She had gone before me in everything, like an older sister. And now, even in death, she went before me. I saw her die but did not see her come before God. But it was no different from her wedding. Just as I trusted in her marriage, I trusted that she had come face to face with Christ. For the first time, I contemplated death. Really and truly dying and standing before God. If Jackie had done it, so would I. I contemplated the purpose of life—to be with our Lord in heaven. I prayed to her, asking her to help prepare me to meet our bridegroom, Christ. Just as she had helped me to enter TAC, helped me to embrace motherhood, I begged her to help me gain heaven.

And she answered my prayers in spades.

MARIPOSA

Walter's career was going very well. Even though he worked long hours, we enjoyed his increased paycheck. With the extra money, we were able to put in a pool, hire a gardener, and have a maid. This was the life! We had so many pool parties, birthday parties, and "just come over" parties! Meanwhile, Walter slowly slipped away, spending more and more time at work. But we were having so much fun, we didn't notice.

It was a gorgeous California fall evening. The children were running around in our neighborhood playing with other children. I was nursing William and enjoying a good book before starting dinner. My husband came home. Early. Very early. I blinked. "Oh. You are home. Hello my love."

He kissed me and fell on the couch. "Where are the kids?" he asked. "I came home early to play with them."

"They are at the neighbors; I'll call them home."

"Matthew? Franz? Your father is home early, time to come home."

"We want to play here, Mom."

Dead. Empty. Silence.

Walter looked at me. His face was crushed. We had long since gotten used to him being gone.

And That. Was the beginning of the end. Or the beginning of the start. Walter got up from the couch and looked at me. "I'm getting a job that is eight to five and wherever that is, we are moving."

82

My world completely fell apart. If I did not have eight children who loved their daddy, I would have left him right there and then. I had padded my life with every material comfort. Family nearby, good friends all around, comforts, tutors for the children, workers for the house—everything I wanted. And my husband was ripping that all away from me.

I spent many nights crying on the couch, in the priest's office, and on my sister's shoulder. But finally. Finally, I realized Walter was right. All my comforts were nothing in comparison to the children needing their father. And I suppose, writing this now, this act of absolute violence on my soul was the first severe right turn I made toward heaven. I turned my back and walked away, and, unlike Lot's wife, did not look back.

Sometime during Advent, Walter went for a job interview with Merced County. I dropped him off at his interview. Then, curious, I drove out of the city into the hills. I found the lovely town of Mariposa, surrounded by green rolling hills, streams, and lovely homes. Memories of our old home flooded back, and I was determined to live here.

After the interview, we went home and accepted the proceeding offer. The following weekend, we came back to Mariposa with our two little girls and a baby to look for a home. They were dressed in sweet, matching dresses, with brushed hair and rosy cheeks. We left the older five at home—thinking three children would be the least scary to any real estate agent.

Our agent executed the classic three-step sale. First the Wreck. Then the Target House. Then the Expensive House.

We followed the agent down a long winding road. Dirt road. With rocks. And giant pits in the earth, large enough to hide an animal. We passed strange-looking homes, with collapsed fencing and hostile signs warning us to go back. We didn't even look at each other, afraid of what we would see in each other's eyes. Stoically, we both looked forward.

We pulled up to an open patch of land. There was a house-looking structure. A man stood outside with half his body under the hood of an old truck. We got out of the car, helping out our pretty girls and I held the baby, hiding the fact that I was shivering in shock. The man pulled himself from the engine, his shirt only covered half his very large belly. He wiped his grease-ridden hands on his shirt, spat on the ground, and said, "I see you brought your varmints." Honestly, if I had had the boys, he could have escaped my dismay. But the pretty blond-haired girls in flower-print dresses. No. Not varmints, indeed.

He held out his hand to Walter, who shook it warmly. The man said, "Let me take you on a tour."

We went inside the home and there sat a panel of folk, sitting on a couch. Just sitting there, all lined up. Next to them was a Christmas tree. They stared at us, and we stared at them. Not a sound was made. The man told us, "We did the floor ourselves." He then showed us the uneven edges without a baseboard and the holes around the toilet. "It's hard to get the knife to cut in a circle." We nodded silently, trying to disguise the horror we felt. Years later, when we put in our own floor and struggled to get the lines straight, we laughed because we understood. But at the time, we had nothing to say.

Then he took us into the garage. It was cold and dark and damp. There was a crib there and a bed. He pointed to a chimney with a hole in it and explained it was a great place to store plastic bags. As we looked around in silence, he told us: "This is where Grandma lived with the baby. One Christmas we went to Vegas and when we came home,

Grandma had died. But this place is so cold and damp, her body didn't decay too much!" He said this with great pride. I felt as if I had walked into a haunted house and could barely breathe.

Then he took us outside. "This mound here, it's where we bury the pets. Ha-ha-ha-ha! It's our pet cemetery." We turned a corner and saw a large circular object. It was about forty feet high. We asked what it was. He puffed out his chest, very proud, and said: "That there is the exhaust fan from the Ahwahnee! I was able to bring it home." Again. No words. Where were we?

We asked about the neighbors. He laughed and said: "They love their mary-wanna. They don't bother you none. Except on a full moon. Then they dance neked and make strange sounds. You'll just have to keep your young-ins inside on those nights." And he laughed again, looking at my girls. I held them close. The agent said cheerfully, "Let's go look at the next place." We could not get in the car fast enough.

The next house was the Target House. It was a newly built home. Sat on a hill alone and clean. There was little doubt in our mind that this was safe. The floors had no gaps, the walls freshly painted. No ghosts of dead grandmothers. Or pets even. Carpets clean. Five acres seemed like a million. We sighed with relief. We did not ask about the well and how much water it produced. Did not ask how the house was heated. Did not ask about property lines. We pretty much just breathed. The Target House did its job.

The Expensive House was...expensive. So expensive that the Target House seemed very reasonable. And thus, the Expensive House also did its job.

We fully expected our house in Santa Paula to sell for a very large amount and sell within days. The market was insane with houses selling within minutes of listing and often for thousands more than asking price. Our lender set the price of our home in Santa Paula and declared that he would buy it at that price if no one else did.

So it came to pass that we bought our new home in Mariposa. We walked into it like two blind mice into a trap. Our tails were soon to meet the knife.

We moved in at the end of January. The agent met us there and gave us our keys. She suggested we check the propane tank. "What? The propane tank? What was that?"

"Oh, your source of all heat—water, air, and stove. You might want to make sure there is gas in it. You also might want to look into buying a wood stove in case the electricity goes out."

"You mean…Heat doesn't come from…" Where does heat come from? In the city, it was just there.

She pointed toward the tank. Ominously. And then left. I wandered over there. Not knowing what I was checking. I finally found a mobile lid, lifted it, and found the meter. My triumph over finding the meter was soon eclipsed by the realization it was at zero. I just stood and stared. It was late January. Snow was expected. If we had no propane, we had no heat. We couldn't cook or take warm showers. And I with eight young children. I called the number on the tank and asked them what could be done. She said she would send out propane next week. I just sat on the floor of our home and cried, the tears making stains on my dirty face.

It did in fact snow, but like a gas tank in a car, thankfully zero didn't mean zero. By using everything sparingly, we made it to Monday, when the delivery man, taking pity on us, arrived first thing in the morning.

And thus it was I learned the great truth about Mariposa. It was harsh, and it was wild, but the people had hearts of gold. In that moment, I promised myself that I and my family would rise to that standard of sacrifice and care for our neighbor and help as much as we were able. For I truly saw the desperate need for neighbor helping neighbor when out alone against the savagery of nature.

CHAPTER 5

Novena of Sorrows

FIRST ATTEMPT FARM

When we moved out to the country, Walter promised me lots of animals. It all seemed so simple. We had saved a bit of money for animals, and we were excited to start our dream. We bought two sheep and thought that like all the sheep in the Bible, they would graze peacefully by the house. We tied a rope from one sheep to the other so they would stay together. Immediately upon their release, they bolted. We stood shocked, not knowing what to do, for they had not acted at all like biblical sheep.

We looked for them and called out to them, but to no avail. That night the coyotes made us shudder as they howled and screamed in bloody glee. The next morning, all we found were the lamb skins still attached to the ropes we had tied them with. The ropes were caught on a low bush. They had circled around the bush in fear as their predators came closer and finally devoured them. We were sobered greatly and did not buy any more sheep.

We bought homing pigeons and put them in a beautiful cage made by Walter. After six months, we let them out, as instructed. We looked in awe as they circled in the sky and then…they flew away. From where they came. And that was the end of the homing pigeons. They did exactly as they were trained to do—fly home.

We bought a horse and, not knowing enough about riding, it nearly killed me. And so, we sold him as well.

The children joined 4-H and signed up to raise animals. We went to the meetings. Meetings that had been run since Mariposa became a county. Meetings run by ancestors, grandparents, aunts, and uncles. The children had grown up raising these animals. Many prided themselves on breeding their own. We knew nothing. And by that, I mean, I had literally never seen a pig or a goat in my life. So, we sat in those meetings. Confused. Lost. Not even knowing what questions to ask.

We bravely made a pigpen. We bought T-posts and wire. But oh…we did not know that Mariposa earth has a thing. It "seizes up" after the rains and turns to cement. We also did not know there was such a thing as a "T-post pounder," which is a very heavy hammer/tube-like thing that helps you smash the post into the ground that has turned to cement. We also did not know the pigs would get big. I mean really big. So, we bought chicken wire, because the cute little twenty-pound creature could still be stopped. We bravely put those T-posts in the ground about one to two inches. And strung the chicken wire around them. The whole contraption could have blown over in the wind. We did not know about "pig fencing"—fencing built specifically for the massive, low weight of pigs. Or even that T-posts came in different strengths. Soon we had two 300-pound pigs running around the yard carrying their pen on their backs. Lucky for us, we had food and they came back to us and lived in an imaginary house in order to eat their food.

That year at the fair, after the judging, we missed the awards ceremony. Somewhere, in all the information given to us, we did not realize this was happening. We did not realize that this was a Very Important Ceremony where not only awards were given to the children but also a time and place to honor the hard-working and well-achieved. We did not realize the incredible insult it was to the community to not be there. Even worse, it was assumed that the insult was intentional, and we as "newcomers" had snubbed not only 4-H but the whole community. We were severely and loudly remonstrated: "Where were you? You think you are too good for us? I was going to buy you a beer and thank you for all your help." We were embarrassed that our ignorance had been an insult to those who had helped us. It would, God help us, be the last time.

After that year, we all sat down as a family. We decided a few rules about living in this town. First of all, no more animals until we figured out what we were doing. Second, we were clearly out of our league in just about every aspect of country life. We needed help. One thing I had seen, living in the country needed a lot of work. On everyone's part. I hoped that if we were cheerful and willing to work hard, maybe, maybe, the townsfolk would accept us, and even more importantly, give us advice on how to live in this hostile land. From that moment on, if anyone needed help and we knew about it, we made every effort to help. If it needed many little hands, we were there as a family. If a job needed a strong back, Walter and the boys were there. From dawn to dusk, if a tree fell on a family's house, or someone needed a "party in a box," the Walls made every effort to be there. With eight children, the power of our family's smiles and strong backs made a huge difference. And in return, we not only began to learn how to live but we also gained many friendships as well. It was a principle that changed our lives and our hearts.

THE CROSS

And now our dear Lord brought us closer into His most loving heart. Up until this time, I had borne suffering with good cheer and courage. Our dear Lord was training me, giving me light crosses and instruction on how to manage them. Like the best of coaches, He gave me incident after incident so that my mind had muscle memory. He gave me beautiful paintings that inspired and inflamed my imagination. He gave me St. Gemma as a most inspiring sister-saint and brought me Jackie as an earthly saint. In her book, St. Gemma records a conversation with our Lord. His words are engraved upon my heart:

> Jesus says to Gemma: I shall be a spouse of blood to you, I will love you, but you must be as one crucified. Prove your love for Me as I have proved My love for you; and do you know how? By suffering pains and crosses without number. You must consider yourself honored when I treat you thus, and when I lead you through thorny and sorrowful paths...and be convinced that if I nail you to the Cross, I love you.

Our Lord also brought me Padre Pio to inspire and help me in my journey:

> Bless the Lord for your suffering and accept to drink the chalice of Gethsemane. Be capable of bearing bitter sufferings during your whole life so you can participate in the sufferings of Christ. Suffering born in a Christian way is the condition that God, the author of all grace and of all the gifts that lead to salvation, has established for granting us glory.

With these dear friends at our side, Walter and I walked through the gates of suffering. Not understanding the cross but only my love for our Lord, I offered my sorrows to Him and trusted in His will.

Our house did not sell in Santa Paula. We said a novena, praying for our house to sell. We did not know it would be a nine-month novena of suffering and fear. The great housing market crash came that January. For nine months we paid double mortgages. We paid for maintenance of the house in Santa Paula, and we paid exorbitant electric bills for a house that had poor insulation and required huge amounts of heating and cooling simply to remain livable in a harsh climate. Our entire salary was consumed by these two houses and so we were left to live on credit cards. I cannot express the horrific feeling of falling deeper and deeper into debt with nothing that could be done to fix it. On top of that, we suffered the humiliation of family and friends telling us to live more frugally. There was nowhere to go but down.

THE UNRAVELING

We looked for a priest to bless our house and finally found one who was available. Usually, a blessing is a prayer of protection against evil as well as an entreaty for good.

> May God's blessing descend abundantly upon this house and upon all who dwell in it. May the grace of the Holy Spirit sanctify everyone. May the most holy name of Jesus grant happiness and blessing in full measure to this house and everything within it. May the holy guardian angels protect all in this house from persecutions of the devil, and one day lead us to our heavenly fatherland. May the blessing of Almighty God, the Father, the Son, and the Holy Spirit descend upon us and remain with us always.

However, this priest stood at the doorway of our home and pronounced that "All may enter who wish." Walt and I looked at each other, our blood cold, it seemed to us as if the demons of hell had been invited to enter and torture us.

It seemed then that our lives began to unravel. One time, all our money was stolen from our bank account. When I went to the bank, they found a handwritten withdrawal slip that said B. Witch. They could not account for how someone had come to the window and written a withdrawal for everything we owned, even having signed the wrong name. Of course they gave us our money back, but we felt the attack.

We tried to plant flowers, vegetables, and grass, but our house had been built on a bed of decomposed granite and so nothing grew.

The house began to fall apart with walls that had been quickly built. Walter incurred the wrath of a political climber who forced Walter out of a job. Our lives were unraveling quicker than a cat pulling on a knitted blanket.

When our house in Santa Paula finally sold, it sold for several hundred thousand dollars less than the asking price. We owed the mortgage company. We owed the credit cards. We were in serious trouble. We contacted the bank and asked if we could do something to restructure our home loan. They told us that in order to qualify for that program, we needed to stop paying our mortgage. I asked for this in writing and received this instruction again. And so, not knowing the depth of fraud, corruption, and lies that were behind the banking systems, we complied. We stopped paying our mortgage, the first and last time we ever didn't pay a bill. And this paved the way for the bank to take back the house. Little did we know how deep and how far the trouble ran.

As the summer heat took its toll on the land, our well ran dry. One cannot understand the gutting fear of turning on a faucet and no water coming out. Of not being able to flush a toilet, wipe a child's face, do dishes, or have water to drink. It is absolutely humbling. It is not for nothing that Christ says, "I am living water." For, without water there is death.

We had a 2,500-gallon water tank that fed the house. For a while, we paid every week for water to be delivered, but it was very expensive and not a long-term solution. Digging a new well was fraught with difficulties and expense. Even if they found water on the first try, it could cost a very large amount to put in a new pump. The real problem, however, was if they did *not* find water. Finding water underground was a scientific guess at best and a psychic guess at worst. At a loss as to what to do, we prayed to Padre Pio, who had been known to bring water from a rock and asked him boldly for a miracle on our land. We so desperately needed water.

Walter and I did what we had always done. Muscle memory coming through the fog of fear. We got on our knees and prayed. We celebrated life and love. We worked as hard as we could. And we prayed: *"The righteous cry out, and the LORD hears them; he delivers them from all their troubles. The LORD is close to the brokenhearted and saves those who are crushed in spirit"* (Psalm 34). The Lord began to knit us together in His heart.

JUST JOY

On September 23, on the Feast Day of Padre Pio, the Lord gave us water. We called out the well-driller to open the well and see what was in the ground. We would start with that. With all the children and mother standing by, a prayer on their lips, he opened up the well. Water gushed out. The man laughed. And he measured. "Not this much water even when I put in the well!" he exclaimed with surprise. We laughed and prayed: "Thank you, Padre Pio. Thank you for bringing water from a rock."

Our ninth child was born. A beautiful healthy boy. We named him Karl, inspired by St. Karl who was the son of a

Polish king and an Austrian queen and a very strong and good saint. We gave our son the middle name of Kephas, which is the name our Lord gave to Peter—it does not simply mean "rock" it means monolith, or tectonic plate. "Upon this rock, I will build my church." And then, one of my favorite and less-known saints, Casimir. Karl Kephas Casimir Wall.

He was scheduled for an induction. February 28. That morning, I sat in the orthodontist's office. The sun shone brightly outside. Snow was forecasted all the way down to the valley floor, but it seemed unlikely. An ambulance driver sat in the orthodontist's waiting room while our daughters had their teeth checked. I told her I was going to the hospital that afternoon to deliver a baby. She looked at me sternly and said: "Look, I don't want to deliver your baby on the side of the road in the middle of a snowstorm. Snow is coming and it will be down to 1,000 feet. Get out of here as soon as you can." I called Walter who was working down in the valley, an hour away. He left the office as soon as he could, picked me up, and off we went. We were going to stay in a hotel so we could be at the hospital at 6 a.m. We hugged our children and told them we were coming home with the best present ever! A new baby brother. We could see them dancing with joy as we drove down the mountain. It began to snow as we drove away and by the time we hit the valley, over five inches had accumulated, and the roads were closed. We made it just in time!

During the labor, the nurses were surprised at our joy. "How is it," they asked, "that after nine children you have so much joy?" We looked at them strangely and said: "Why, all we have left is joy! With so many children, we have already gone through all the stress, all the fear, and all the exhaustion. Now. Just joy."

A PIG AND A DUCK

Every fall, Mariposa has a fair. This fair is remarkable, not only because the entire community comes out for four days to laugh, talk, eat, and play, but because of the animal auction. The children spend a large part of the year raising animals and then sell them at the auction. The whole community comes together to support the children and bid on the animals. The bids range in the outrageous, always in the hundreds and sometimes in the thousands. Far, far above market price. This is unique to Mariposa, at least within the surrounding communities. I asked a friend and business owner about it once. He said: "When I was young, the local businesses bought my pigs every year. I saved the money and was able to buy my first truck. With that truck, I was able to start my own business. And now, this is a way for me to give back to the community."

This incredible young man spent thousands on different animals supporting the children of Mariposa, mine included. For many, the money paid for the first year of college, or a first car, or perhaps an investment in a new line of breeding animal. It is an amazing event.

Franz decided that year to show a pig at the fair. He invested a large amount of money into the pig and caring for it properly. However, that summer, there was a terrible heat wave. Friends came to visit and while we sat in the cool house, there was a pig outside suffering. We did not know. They asked to see the pigs, and when we all went out, we discovered the pig had died.

We were in shock with guilt and grief, but most urgent, we had to do something with the pig carcass. The ground was so hard that we could not bury it. So, we all helped to put the 250-pound animal into the wheelbarrow, and then all helped to push that heavy, dead weight up the mountain in order to dump it in the ravine.

That night it was quiet. We knew who had the animal. A mountain lion. All the earth is afraid of that king and is silenced, even the crickets. And when we heard its scream, the scream like a woman that makes you shudder even in your bed, we knew it had been challenged over its meal and that was not to be. Terror ran up and down our spine and we were happy for the strong walls of our house.

It went out to the community that Franz's pig had died. Everyone understood the investment and heartache that went along with this tragedy. We received a phone call from a very kind woman. "I am with 4-H Poultry. I have an extra duck I can give you. I will help you raise it, and maybe you can get some of your investment back." We accepted her offer. She helped us build a pen for our duck and taught us how to raise it. Well, that duck won Grand Champion, and Franz earned everything he had lost, plus some. We gave a check to that wonderful woman and thanked her with tears in our eyes. God sent us an angel and we would never forget.

ANGELS AMONG US

At the end of this tumultuous year, my sister came out to visit with her young children. It was a wonderful time until my two-year-old son, William, ran off with his two-year-old cousin. They were lost in the wilds behind the house. We called the police and immediately the property was swarmed with Search and Rescue, the sheriff's department, friends, neighbors, and football coaches. The air was full of helicopters. We lived in a very dangerous place, full of old mining shafts, deep ravines, and a mountain lion. It seemed as if the entire town came out to help us. Finally, my sister's son was found. All he could say was "William is stuck." But they could not find William. One sherriff's deputy came to me and said, "If we don't find him before dark…" I knew. We had seen the sheep; we had heard the lion.

We were on our knees praying. I was overwhelmed by the generosity and kindness of the people in the town, from nearly every walk of life. They were all here to help find my son. I was sick with fear.

Walter rushed home from work. He paused and said a prayer. He had a clear and forceful thought. "Go in this direction." He told a nearby officer who laughed at him and said, "We've already been there." A young man with the Probation Department spoke up: "Hey, this is the father. If he says to go here, we will."

So, two deputies and Walter went in a fan-like formation. They found William deep in the bushes, stuck on a barbed-wire fence. The fence had been built on the edge of a cliff to keep the cows from going off the sharp ravine on the other side. It had saved William's life. When Walter rushed to pick him up, William looked back and said, "Bye, friend."

We tried to ask William what had happened, but at the age of two he could not speak. I knew that at a certain time, the curtain of forgetfulness would wipe out all memories. I was in a panic to find out what happened before he forgot everything. Would he speak before the curtain closed?

We waited a long time to find out what happened. William could not talk at three or even four years of age. I signed him up for speech therapy, not understanding why he wouldn't speak. Finally, at the age of five, when Karl took his cars away, William exclaimed, "Karl! Give me back my cars!" I canceled the speech therapist. William, having seven brothers and sisters taking care of him, anticipating his needs, and loving on him, just hadn't found a reason to speak. It wasn't until his younger brother took his cars away that William spoke up and continued to speak, most eloquently.

I waited for a quiet moment during the day and then asked him, "William, what happened when you were lost?" He smiled his large, compelling smile, and began:

"Leon and I went out for a walk. I got stuck and Leon went home to get help. Helicopters came and shouted out my name. I thought they were bad, so I hid. Then an angel came and sat with me. He told me not to be scared and he would bring my daddy. He was very nice, and we sat for a long time and talked. The angel told me many things. Then Daddy came and told the helicopters to go away. I said goodbye to my friend."

"Do you see angels around us?" I asked.

"Yes, Mama. There are always angels around us."

NOVENA OF SUFFERING

While fighting the banks and watching our resources shrivel to nothing, I became pregnant with our tenth child. Always overjoyed with new life, we celebrated. However, after a few months, I had a miscarriage. And Walter had a heart attack. His heart simply broke. I told the family the baby's name was Sophia, "Wisdom." We did not know if it was a boy or a girl, but I did know it was a mother's right to name the baby within her womb.

I wrote a Novena of Sorrows. Scared. Willing. Trusting.

She was an unwilling bride. Understanding that His embrace was her destiny yet she was fearful. Like a frightened animal afraid of the outstretched hand. Afraid of the unknown. What, she wonders, is the price of submission? She will abandon her freedom, her independence, her will—and for what? For Him. He is her groom. Her mother takes her by the hand, caresses her hair, and whispers sweet words of encouragement and wisdom. She brings her daughter to the bridal chamber. Their friends and family surround its brightly decorated walls. Encouraging. Rejoicing in the marriage of bride and groom. He takes her by the hand, His—scarred and wounded, hers—fresh and delicate, without mark. She knows that God is a loving God, and suffering is His marriage bed. She turns to our mother for help, because she alone can give us the grace to remain with Him. And at last, she understands that God is a loving God, and her joy is with Him. Even if it is the cross.

Meanwhile, we decided, upon torturous deliberation and prayer, to file for bankruptcy. As this process was going on, I became pregnant again. This baby made it through the first three months, and we were full of hope. I told Walter her name was Clara. He looked at me sadly and said: "Don't name her Clara. That is the name of the sick girl in *A Secret Garden*. Name her Claire." My face grew white as ash and I said slowly, "I think she *is* sick." There was a moment of profound silence and Walter led the family in a little prayer.

***

CLARA

The baby was due in June. I went for my first ultrasound in January.

As the nurse prepared the ultrasound wand, I could feel my baby fluttering and kicking in my womb. One of my favorite parts of pregnancy was having the first ultrasound. There is always that moment when the baby suddenly lights up the ultrasound screen. That moment when darkness turns to light and new life suddenly is known. I waited with happy expectation. "It is a girl," the nurse said with a smile. My daughter. My daughter, Clara. It was music to my ears to say her name. As she turned in my womb, I could almost see her pretty face laughing. I was breathless with her beauty.

The nurse's eyes suddenly grew sad, and I saw it in an instant. She folded the sheet over my belly solemnly and told me she needed to bring in the doctor. I could barely breathe as I waited.

The doctor took the ultrasound wand and looked at my baby. "It looks like she has trisomy 18." I could not process her words for they were unfamiliar and had no meaning. I looked on the ultrasound screen, looking for proof that the doctor was wrong. I was so enamored with her pretty little round head that I did not see the horrendous cysts taking up the space where her brain ought to be. Her arms waved in front of the camera like a sweet greeting and my heart swelled with love, but I did not see that the other one lay floating, for it had no bones. "The misty floaty thing," the technician said to me, as I admired my daughter's curved spine, "is her bowels." I could not even process this information. For she had taken off again in a flight of fancy, swirling and leaping in joy. And finally, the technician explained that her heart was doing nothing because it was broken. I looked at the technician with wide eyes and said, "But my heart is all she needs."

"Yes," she agreed slowly. "But your baby will die once she leaves your womb. Do you want to abort the pregnancy?"

Tears filled my eyes. I could only think: "My little daughter is alive and rejoicing in life. She knows my voice, the beating of my heart, the measure of my step. She knows the deep voice of her father, the laughing voices of her nine brothers and sisters. My womb is giving her the only life she will ever know, the minute she is born, the world will kill her. Every moment within my womb is a moment of joy and love and comfort that she would not otherwise have." What mother does not wish to protect her child with her very body? I was given the unique privilege of giving her the only life and protection she would ever know. I shook my head "no" and told her firmly, "I do not want an abortion."

She helped me off the bed, and then, overcome with grief, I ran to the bathroom. Collapsing, I fell on the floor before the door and crawled into the bathroom. I cried so hard, I passed out. A doctor brought me out of the bathroom and into a room. "Can you call your husband to bring you home?" I shook my head, "No. He is in trial and cannot leave." I had to drive the long hour and a half home. I pulled over and cried many times and finally made it home. Only to tell the excited children that their sister would die. It was only by the grace of God that I made it through that night.

And so, I carried her in my womb. Rejoicing in her movement. Knowing she could hear my voice. Knowing she could hear her brothers and sisters. Analise, at the age of five, wrote a beautiful piece of music. She named it "Clara's Song" and played it for me while I rested. Clara danced in my womb. How she loved that song. She could hear the boys shouting and playing, and the older kids discussing their school. She loved to hear her daddy's voice when he came home in the evenings, deep and resonant.

But there was a problem. Her heart could not pump blood because it was broken. She could not process the water in my womb because she was broken. And so, my heart grew increasingly weary and my womb increasingly heavy with water. I was in danger of rupture and a heart attack. This was in February, and she was not due until June. We spoke to doctors, and of course the answer was an abortion. This I could not do. I could not stop the beautiful vibrant life that existed only in my womb. Another answer was to move near the hospital because Mariposa was over an hour away from the hospital. With eight young children, I could not do this either. And so, we prayed.

Late in February, I cried silent tears while Walter slept. He had a difficult case against a man who had beaten an elderly woman nearly to death. This man had demons tattooed on his arm that told him what to do. I had to let Walter sleep. I prayed for my husband through my gasping tears.

I suddenly felt a great peace. I knew with complete faith that I would be all right, and my body would hold Clara safely as long as she needed. I fell into a deep and peaceful sleep.

March came. I knew that Clara was not doing well. Her times of movement were less and less. My heart was breaking every day a little more. And then there came a night. I had a dream. I was holding a little baby. She was about four months old and fat and wriggly. I could smell her hair and feel her soft skin in my arms. Our Lord held out His hands and asked me for her. "Will you give her to me? Will you offer your suffering for the salvation of souls?" I hugged the baby closer and breathed deeply her fragrance. She wrapped her little arms around me and snuggled her face to my face. And then I looked at my Lord, my lover. I handed Him my pretty little girl.

I was sobbing. Even in my sleep. Walter woke me up and I was wild with grief. "She's gone," I gasped. "She died."

"How do you know?"

I told him about the dream. He told me, "Go to the doctor first thing in the morning and find out." At the doctor's office, she confirmed my baby had died in the middle of the night.

Giving birth to a dead baby was the worst and hardest thing I have ever done. I had no family with me. Just Walter and me in a darkened room. It was a Friday in Lent. And we joined Christ in His crucifixion.

When she was born, Walter had the incredible inspiration to take my baby and place her in my arms. I held her to my heart and nuzzled her face. She was warm and smelled like me. We looked at her arm, which had no bones. Felt the soft part of her skull where there was no brain. We tucked her intestines close to her body and wrapped her in a blanket. She was beautiful. Absolutely perfect. She looked like a Wall. One of the fiery ones, with black hair and dark eyelashes. That single moment, holding my baby, was the difference between insanity and grief. She was mine and I knew her. My breasts swelled up with milk, ready to nurse her. It took ten years for my body to let go of that milk. Ten years to stop waiting for her to be brought back to me.

And then, the most horrible moment. I handed my warm, fragrant baby to the nurse. She was to be put in the freezer.

Walking out of the hospital without my baby…I have no words to describe the pain and aching loneliness. I could only think of the brave girls who gave their babies up for adoption and those who were lied to and ordered the death of their child. I prayed for those girls. Both of those girls. And offered my broken heart for theirs.

We had a beautiful funeral, with many dear friends from both Mariposa and Santa Paula. During the funeral, William laughed. I looked at him. "William, why did you laugh?"

"Clara is here, Mama, and she is playing with me." I looked at him in wonder.

THE GIRL IN GOLD

There was now a great sorrow in our hearts. I was thrown into the worst grief I had ever experienced. All I wanted was to be with my child—even if it meant crawling in that grave. I had no consolation and no comfort.

At one point, I went to confession and confessed anger toward God and a lack of faith. "How do I know God loves me?" I asked. "Why would He take Clara if He loved me?"

And the priest said the most profound thing that could have been said to me. "Look at the cross," he said. "That is how you know He loves you."

And in a single blinding moment, I understood why we have an image of the crucified Lord on the cross. Not because "He is stuck there" as some claim. No. It is so that we never forget the sacrifice our Lord made for us. It is so we never forget that He loves us unto death. I contemplated the cross for many hours and many days.

And then something happened. I found joy. It came as a surprise. The birth of a baby goat. A field of flowers. My children playing in a pond. My husband's kindness, or a child's gift. The sound of laughing as my children played with newborn puppies. It came in bright relief, stronger and deeper than I had ever known. For in contrast to that deep gulf of grief, joy was a bright light. Suddenly, I found myself in those paintings that had seared my heart so, so long ago: longing, love, sorrow, joy, battle, and peace. All of this raging within my heart, seeking its own place, settling into place.

But there was another, deeper transformation within my heart. Having carried such sorrow, I found the capacity for a profound sympathy toward those who were wounded. What that girl in a gold dress lacked, our Lord had now shown me. Compassion. Understanding. My sorrow, which nearly killed me, was a means by which I could understand others' sorrow. And pray for them. My sorrow was a bridge to love. My heart hurt for them and so I was able to walk with them, if only in part, on their journey of suffering. It was as if, in the breaking of my heart, my love spilled out from myself into the world. And now a deep and longing passion grew within my heart to love and protect the people of Mariposa. It was a grace, unbidden and a surprise. But it was there, and my heart was stamped with love for those around me. And so, the advice of the girl in gold, so long ago, came back to me, "Let the sorrow bring you closer to Christ, offer up your suffering to Christ for the salvation of souls." And I found the advice to be true and pure.

Though I was grateful to walk in that sorrow and learn all it was meant to teach me, I did not know a greater sorrow was yet to come. A sorrow that would rend me like the great curtain in the temple but would allow me the great privilege of joining Our Lady on her Via Dolorosa.

We all felt Clara's presence and love upon us, illuminating joy and making way the path to heaven. For if she was in heaven, so would I be. And all my family. I would do everything in my power to reunite my family under the gaze of our Lord. I began to see that she could do more good in heaven than on earth. I began to understand that I had done my job as a mother to Clara, and now she was in heaven, fully alive and carrying out good upon earth. We felt her presence more and more as did, strangely enough, others. Joy, like gold light, falling where Clara fluttered.

Clara died on March 9, and ten days later on the Feast Day of St. Joseph, March 19, our bankruptcy was approved and finalized. They came to take our home and our car. We were left with the clothes on our back and the van—because that is what they left you. One car and your clothing.

I was not sad to leave our house. It seemed to me it was a house that should not have been. It was made quickly in the housing insanity, made to flip, and make money. Not made for generations. It was carved out of a hill with not enough water and not enough earth. Sitting on the gravel like an impostor. It had seen too much death and too much sorrow. As soon as we left, the well ran dry. The miracle of water reserved for that little family circled in love and prayer. No, I was not sad to leave.

<hr />

OUR LADY OF GUADALUPE

But therein lay the problem. The deep and serious problem. There was nowhere to go. There was no room at the inn. It was December and we had to be out of our home by December 22—three days before Christmas. The government had no calendar other than its own. We prayed a novena to Our Lady of Guadalupe, begging her for a place to lay our heads. "In and through her sorrow of not having a home to lay your Son's head, please, sweet Lady, give my children a home."

There was only one rental in Mariposa large enough to be legally rented to a family of our size. It was huge with three stories, overlooking the fields. A beautiful house, hand built by a father of a large family. It sat below the snowline at around 1,500 feet, with grassy fields and a huge barn.

...And it was overrun with meth addicts and squatters. We went to see the house with the real estate agent. But in this house were piles of trash so high they overtook the ceiling. Rotting food, animal waste, human waste. It was the most horrifying sight I had ever seen. But alas, there were rules about evicting them. The owner could not turn off electricity or use any other coercion. If we could not rent that house, we would have to leave Mariposa. It was as simple as that. We had fallen in love with Mariposa and did not want to leave.

On the night of December 12, the Feast of Our Lady of Guadalupe, we were at our friend's house, who lived close by to this big house. Suddenly our daughters started screaming! It was snowing! Over fifteen years they had lived there, and it had never snowed. We built up the fire and enjoyed a cozy evening with our friends. After an hour, the electricity went out. Walter had an idea. "I'm just going to go check on the house," he said. "It is the last day of the novena." We didn't even tell our friends what the novena was about. Our hearts were in our throats. We had come to love the incredible community and natural virtue of our friends.

Walter drove away. In a little while, he came back. His face was radiant and beaming. "They are gone!" he shouted. "The snow and loss of electricity made them leave! They are gone!" We cried and screamed and laughed with joy! Our sweet Lady! We would have a home to live in. We could stay in Mariposa!

SOJOURNERS

We spoke with the owner of the home and told him that we had filed for bankruptcy, but that in a few years we would like to buy the home. He happily agreed.

However, the home had a few problems. There was no insulation and so in the winter, the house was bitter cold. So cold, one had to wear mittens and ski hats. And in the summer it was so hot that we walked around with red faces, sweating. In the winter, the barn flooded because it was at the base of a hill that drained all the rainwater into the barn. The electricity had a "leak," and our bill was over a thousand dollars in a single month. The renting agency tried its best to fix these things, but the owner of the property was not willing to spend the money to actually fix it. Still, we had high hopes of buying the house and fixing all the problems.

Meanwhile, I became pregnant once again. This pregnancy was very dangerous for me. I was very sick and started to lose my hair and had no color. At one point, I got poison oak, but it manifested itself in large blood blisters all over my body. When I went to the dermatologist, he nearly passed out with how horrible they were. He said there was nothing he could do and sent me home. We were trying to build up our credit, save money, and manage a complicated house, and it all took a drastic toll on my health.

Walter named the baby Emma. And so, when she too passed through the walls into eternity, she had a name. Once, Walter was in his study and a book spontaneously fell to the floor. It was *Emma* by Jane Austin. He knew that it was Emma playing with him and that she was happy.

Then, after a year of sorrow and struggle, there appeared a note on the door. It came out of nowhere, like an impostor, unbidden. The note was brief and to the point. The house was being auctioned and we had thirty days to leave. No warning by the owner. Just. Leave.

Our credit was still in lockdown from the bankruptcy and we knew there was nowhere else to go. We prayed. And we asked Clara to ask our Lord to help us.

We talked to my parents about the possibility of them buying a home until our credit cleared and we could buy it back from them. They agreed but could only afford a very small loan. This left most of the housing market out of reach. We prayed and prayed.

We found a home that was on a popular auction site. It was a gorgeous piece of property with a rotting cabin on it. The starting auction price was $30,000, and we thought we could buy it for that, demo the cabin, and build a new home. We talked to our parents and they, having built a home themselves, were very doubtful.

We waited for the day it went for auction. We watched in absolute disbelief as the home had increased bids—again and again. It finally sold for over $200,000! Did they not realize there was *no home*! This puzzled us enough to look into the auction process. During this time the auction company was sued because it was raising the bid itself to artificially inflate the cost of the homes it was trying to sell. It was astonishing the corruption involved in the housing market. This was at the same time many large banks were being sued for telling folks to not pay their mortgage in order to have legal cause to confiscate their home.

We spent those thirty days frantically looking for a home. Meanwhile, we talked to the rental agency, and we managed to secure another sixty days in our home before we had to leave. But the clock was ticking before a family with nine young children had nowhere to live.

CHAPTER 6

A Time of Joy

CLARA'S MIRACLE

We very much felt the presence of Clara in our lives. The children would spontaneously say "Clara is with us!" Or "I feel Clara's presence." We thought of her as our little Mariposa, or our little butterfly. When we saw a butterfly, we would think she was with us. We decided to ask her to intercede for us in finding a home. She, who was with our Lord, and yet knew so intimately the daily life in our home.

We scoured the ads for homes for sale or rent. We visited some homes. Homes high on hills with nearly undrivable roads, homes with lots of land but all of it unusable due to high terrain or thick brush. Everything was expensive and nothing was right. Walter began to study the topography of Mariposa and determined that Bear Valley was the closest to town and the closest to Merced, where he worked. He determined, furthermore, that it had the nicest land. Rolling hills, streams, large oak trees, and large places of open pasture. So, when he found a property in Bear Valley on the market, he could not contain his joy. He showed me the picture. It was a home on cinder blocks, surrounded by trash. I could not look further. I could still smell the stench of rot left by the squatters. I knew I did not have the stomach or the money to clean up a home in such absolute wreckage. And so, I put him off.

Finally, as an anniversary gift to Walter, I agreed to go out and see this property. He had not stopped talking about how wonderful it was and how it perfectly suited us.

I drove out to the house. I was sick with fear of what I would see and sat silently in the car as Walter explained how perfectly the house was situated. We drove into the property, along a lovely winding road and came upon the house. To my astonishment, the trash was gone. It was a simple house sitting proudly on a gentle hill. All around were fields with grass. Good earth producing good grass. The home was surrounded by beautiful mountains. The little town was quiet and peaceful.

We walked in the house. Though humble and small on the outside, inside it was open and light. There were three very small bedrooms but there were cathedral ceilings in the living room, which begged for a crucifix. There was a second living room with large floor-to-ceiling windows that gazed out upon a beautiful pasture gently falling away from the house and tumbling into a stream. I had one thought. "This will do."

The smile and look of wonder on my face said everything to Walter. He took my hand and said, "Let's walk out back, shall we?"

We walked out behind the house. Forty acres of beauty after beauty. Each turn of the path revealing another breathtaking scene. A stream that flowed through beautiful dark granite rocks; open fields spotted with huge, old oak trees; small swimming holes surrounded by beautiful, black, sleek, granite walls, just waiting for the frolic of children. And as we hiked the last hill, we turned in wonder. There before us, we watched the sun play upon the mountains, turning pink and lighting up in golden light. Suddenly, it began to lightly snow. Soft, languid flakes, covering the earth in white. We knew this was a snow blessing, brought by our Lady to purify the land. Our hearts were so on fire with love of the property, we could barely contain ourselves. We flew down the mountain and called my parents.

It was on the market for $180,000. My parents put down an offer of $170,000. Nothing happened. So, they upped the offer to full asking price. Still, nothing happened. Prayers and desperate novenas flew from our mouths and hearts. Even more so as the ticking clock to eviction relentlessly continued on.

One Saturday, I was at a friend's house, and her husband suddenly said: "Hon, remember that property I was looking at? It's being auctioned!" My friend smiled at me indulgently. Her husband loved to watch properties. Curious, I looked over his shoulder and saw it was *our* property! The very one we had put on an offer! Too stunned to say much, I begged my departure and flew home. I tore in the door shouting, "Walter! It's being auctioned!" We went to the computer and verified that it was indeed. We called my mother and told her. We all looked again. Starting bid was $35,000. But there, in small print, were the words "must have insurance before bidding."

We began to call around looking for a company to insure it. And therein lay the problem. Therein lay why no one had bought this piece of heaven. Insurance companies would not insure a mobile home. Especially one in foreclosure. We finally heard from a friend of a friend of a company that insured motorcycles (of all things). They also insured motorcycle trailers and, by extension, trailers that were used to live in. Done deal! We secured insurance and then went to look at what it took to bid.

A deposit of $10,000. A good faith deposit to a company prosecuted for fraud. We were all sick, especially my mother who is extremely fiscally prudent and cautious. We researched how to use the auction correctly and how to avoid its fraud. We talked and prayed all weekend. And finally, Monday morning, the day before the auction, my mother came home from Mass and said: "Clara told me to do it. She told me to bid on the property." I sucked in my breath and tried not to pass out with total and absolute joy.

We discussed our plan. We would bid on the property but not go higher than $190,000. If the reserve had not been met by then, we would let it go.

Tuesday morning. The day of the auction. My mother bravely sent in the $10,000 deposit, knowing it was possibly gone forever. And then we bid. Our internet was slow. It took about five minutes for the bid to register and for "Reserve Not Met" to show up. We figured the reserve would be the asking price of $180,000 when it was on the market.

First bid, $35,000. Reserve Not Met.

Second bid, in increments of $10,000, $45,000. Reserve Not Met.

Hit the button again. And again. Let's get to the exciting part. Push the button again.

Now it's time for my mom to go to Mass. We were at $85,000, "Reserve Not Met."

"Should I go?" she asked. "What if someone else bids?"

"Mom, go to Mass. Pray. Ask Clara. This is in God's hands."

The line went quiet, and I stared at the screen. Suddenly the bids started moving again. I saw the numbers going up. I looked, sick at heart. But it was my mom's bid, catching up! They finally stopped at $135,000, "RESERVE MET." I nearly screamed with excitement! Who would have thought that with an offer still on the table of $180,000, the reserve would be lower than that at $135,000! Furthermore, if my mom had not stopped bidding to go to Mass, we would have inadvertently kept bidding above the reserve! Later, we heard rumors that the auction company was sued for programming into the system a lag time between bid and record of the bid. This caused bidders to lose track of how their bids corresponded to price. Our Lord had preserved us.

As soon as my mom came home from Mass, she called and I told her the news, nearly crying with joy and now sick with stress. Would they do what they were notorious for doing? Bid up the price? Would someone else bid on this wonderful piece of heaven? My mom and I stared at the computer all day. Walter came home early, and he too stared at it. We prayed every moment of that day.

The bid did not move!

Not another soul bid on that property and we got it for the reserve price of $135,000 while still having an offer in the stratosphere of $180,000!

Clara gave her mom and dad a new home for an incredibly low price.

LIVINGSTONE FARM

Peter 2:5: *"Be you also, like living stones, are being built into a spiritual house to be a holy priesthood, offering spiritual sacrifices acceptable to God through Jesus Christ."*

The thirty-day escrow corresponded almost to the day of our eviction. Just in time. Just in God's time.

We started to pack up and move. But here was the rub. The big, gigantic rub. The house was one-third of the size of the one we were living in. And there were no fences. No barns. No garage.

Just a simple house on a piece of land.

We could not gain entry until escrow closed. So, it turned out that we had two days in between escrow closing and eviction from the other house. Talk about a rock and a hard place. We packed as much as we could before the move date.

When the starting bell rang, it was all hands on deck. Walter and the older kids packed our family van and a moving van and drove to the new house. They unloaded it on the driveway and went back again. I was watching children and packing the old house. I did not know what was going on at the new house. Did not know that every belonging I owned, including clothing and beds, was on the driveway because the men were in a hard rush to make so many trips. At a certain point, as the weekend drew to a close and we had run out of time, Walter and the boys were raking and shoveling things from one house, onto a flatbed truck we borrowed from a friend, onto the driveway of the other house.

All the while, another set of boys was busy building a pen for all our animals: a steer, goats, chickens, and a dog.

On Sunday, they brought me to the new house. I cried. I sat down and cried. We made it out of the old house, sure enough, and just in time. But oh. Seeing everything I loved on the road like belongings tossed aside with no regard. My heart was gutted.

"No problem, Mama, we will get it all sorted out."

We worked tirelessly to put up a shed, and to get the beds and clothing into the house. But, oh, it was a small house. A few beds had nowhere to go. Lots of dressers found no homes. Some clothing and jackets found no place in a closet.

And then it rained. A hard, glorious spring rain. All those items outside were ruined. Molded. The grass grew five feet in what seemed like days. I have a picture of what looks like an entire household covered by grass, and all of it ruined. It had to be thrown away. Some have asked me, "Was it freeing to get rid of your stuff?" No. It was heartbreaking. We had so little as it was, and everything we owned was precious to us. Precious like "My precious." (*Lord of the Rings*) Maybe. And maybe that was why God took it away. But it hurt. And I was sad.

We finally built quadruple bunk beds and got four kids to a room. We stacked dressers one on top of the other. We put in two rows of closet bars. We added a bookcase to any blank wall we had. And finally, finally, we found some sort of living arrangement that worked.

The first thing we did was beg our dear friend and holy priest from Santa Paula to come and bless the house. He drove five hours and gave it a proper blessing and casting away of evil spirits. It was the first time our home in Mariposa had been blessed and we all sighed in deep contentment.

We were going to be OK. We were blessed. And we were living in the most beautiful place we had ever seen. Clara had worked her miracle and found a beautiful home for her family.

PICK UP YOUR CROSS

One afternoon, I was sitting in the afternoon sun, resting, and praying, I looked up at the picture our friends had given us as we left Santa Paula. It was a disturbing picture of Christ carrying His cross. It had always bothered me that this was their going-away present. Christ looked very tortured and sad and it seemed like an ominous gift.

But, as I had looked at it so many times and thought of how it had been a foreshadowing of all our sorrows, I had a different thought on this day. There was a song on the radio about a soldier who "picks up his gun and goes back to work." The song sang about the irony of a battle being a daily job like going to the office. But it struck me that we also have a battle daily and that our "gun," our weapon, is the cross. Having endured so much suffering, I began to understand the power that suffering had against evil. And that every cross, every sorrow united with our Lord, was an attack against Satan and a means by which grace enters the world. I began to think very practically about offering up suffering to God for the salvation of souls.

I read the saints' stories and learned from them, like a hungry student. During Mass, I contemplated the presence of the angels adoring the Real Presence of Christ in the

Eucharist. I saw how the saints offered up their sorrows. I learned the importance of obedience, because it is by their own willfulness that our original mother and father went astray and so easily do we, as well.

I began to understand the importance of time, and that every moment of our daily life can be used in adoring God, being kind, or just asking, "Lord, what would You have me do?"

And, because all grace is outflowing, we began to pray about how to bring grace to our community. We stumbled upon the daily meditations of Josemaria Escriva and prayed deeply about how to live our faith in a real and true way. The passion for the salvation of souls did not waver, and we spoke about it as a family. How can we help those around us? How can we love them?

I began to notice that when I was given a cross, it would soon happen that I would talk to a friend who had been given a similar cross. And as I commiserated and consoled my friend, I realized I would not have had either the compassion or any words of wisdom had I not just experienced the same cross. And so, I began to understand the economy of suffering. That God gives us suffering so that we can love others more.

Mother Teresa was our constant inspiration. Her acceptance of a Nobel Peace Prize became our guidepost for loving those around us.

> I will never forget when I brought a man from the street. He was covered with maggots; his face was the only place that was clean. And yet that man, when we brought him to our home for the dying, he said just one sentence: I have lived like

an animal in the street, but I am going to die like an angel, loved, and cared for, and he died beautifully. He went home to God, for death is nothing but going home to God. And he, having enjoyed that love, that being wanted, that being loved, that being somebody to somebody at the last moment, brought that joy in his life. (Nobel acceptance speech on December 10, 1979)

We tried our best to love, respect, and care for each person who God brought into our life. We are human and so we failed. We are selfish, tired, and proud. But this example of love was our guide and inspiration. And if it took suffering to help in that care, I was beginning to trust in God's ability to give me just what I could handle. And, as Mother Teresa said, "God doesn't require us to succeed, He only requires that you try." And try we did.

We talked to our children about this responsibility. We had many conversations about why people behaved the way they did and how we could avoid participation in evil but also not judge the person. We talked about why things were right or wrong and talked about how to keep friendships with those who thought differently than us but whom we loved and respected for their natural virtue.

And so it was that we tried our best to live well and offer every sorrow and cross up to our sweet Lord, for the salvation of souls, first and foremost our own.

MARIPOSA STRONG

As we became more and more involved in the community, we began to know our fellow Mariposans better. We were overwhelmed by their loyalty, kindness, natural virtue, and insight. We were inspired by their love of all the children in the community, their desire to help them grow in virtue and strength, and then to go out in the world to succeed. This love and support for the children was evident in the many sports programs, the 4-H programs, as well as in the schools. The children were regarded as the greatest treasure of the community. They were supported, encouraged, and guided toward not only natural virtue but material success.

We were inspired by their hard work ethic, their love of animals, their awareness of nature, and finally, their reverence for God. For as anyone who works with the earth, there is a great natural humility in the face of God. They must depend on Him for weather, for help with animals, and for most every aspect of their lives. Furthermore, they recognized the deep need for a strong community spirit because in the face of calamity, each one needed help from neighbors.

And this is why, when William was lost, nearly the whole town came out to look. I had only seen dimly what we were beginning to see deeply. The profound spirit of community and love of neighbor that overrode all politics and diversity of culture.

And yet, I could not have guessed how the town would come together to support Franz. I could not have imagined that the town would rally behind our family and do everything it could to help us. And after eight months of fighting for his life, when it was finally time to come home, this beautiful town would line the streets with signs of love and encouragement, even giving my son the honor of a sheriff's escort when we crossed into Mariposa County. No, I was only just beginning to see the immense love, kindness, and incredible character this town had as a community.

God blessed our family with many good friends. The kind of friends who would die for you, who were loyal and kind. They brought us beauty, laughter, and wisdom. Each of them a jewel; unique, bright, and beautiful.

I will never forget, one hot, windy summer day, I looked up from my place at the pool where I was working as a lifeguard and swim teacher. I saw a cloud of smoke. I looked anxiously and then went back to watching the children swim. At break, I looked again, the cloud of smoke was starting to fill the sky. I checked my phone for fire updates and was immediately overwhelmed with the many messages from friends all over Mariposa County. "I can take your horses." "I can take your ducks and geese." "I can take your pigs." "… your goats…" And best of all, "I have an Airbnb that can sleep eleven, it is yours if you need it." On and on. Messages piling upon messages. Stunned with their generosity, I deliberated what to do. Did we need to evacuate? How much time did we have? I looked again at the sky. The wind was high and the fire close and I knew it was time to take action.

I begged leave with the other lifeguards and drove home to a conflagration bearing down on our little town of Bear Valley. I relayed the offers of help to my family, and we jumped into action to evacuate our home. Some friends showed up to help, and others with small children came asking for help. I sent the older boys to help with other neighbors and my girls went to help Search and Rescue with evacuations. Everyone plugged the Airbnb address into their phones, and we promised to all be there before the dawn. Within hours, our small section of the county had evacuated thanks only to the community working together.

That fire, the Detwiler Fire, was one of the largest in our area, covering most of the county by the time it was put out. Because of the immense community response, very few homes were burnt and there were no casualties. The community banded together, neighbor helping neighbor, and we came out of that disaster with strength and spirit.

And so it was that I was taught through these amazing people the love of neighbor and the value of natural virtue. I saw firsthand that the salt of the earth had not gone flat. I was even more inspired to take on suffering so that I could give back to my town of Mariposa the great miracle of love its people had given to me. "Never worry about numbers. Help one person at a time and always start with the person nearest you," said Mother Teresa. We were learning.

SERENGETI SEVEN

At the lowest point in my grief after Clara's death, I had a thought while praying before the cross. "I will send you a horse, a special horse, who will help you through this grief. You will know this horse because it will be a paint" (a horse that has a spotted pattern). I was excited about this and looked at many paint horses to buy. But none of them seemed right. Then my friend told me she had a horse someone was trying to sell. Did I want to come look at it? Of course, I did!

I went to the horse pen where a beautiful golden horse circled around wildly, screaming, and rearing. He was amazing and beautiful in his wildness. I walked up slowly, with my arms behind my back. I stood at the gate quietly. He bolted to the furthest corner and snorted, head held high, nostrils flaring, eyes wide with fear. I put my eyes down and was quiet. My body was so grief-ridden; it was no threat. He took a step forward. I barely dared to look at him, he was so magnificent. Arched neck and flashing hooves, he came closer. I was in one of those paintings in France, standing in front of a fierce war horse. I trembled. And then I felt it, a warm breath on my face. I inhaled his warm fragrant breath. And when I exhaled, he breathed in, receiving my breath. I looked up into his eyes, and they were soft. He put his nose on my shoulder and rested. I knew. Paint or no paint, this was the horse given to me by God for the healing of my soul.

And when I saw his pedigree, I could only gasp. The sire of this horse was an albino paint. A secret paint. Hidden from all the world, except for me. He was mine.

I named him Serengeti Seven. Seven for heaven. Seven for the seven deadly sins and the seven heavenly virtues. Seven because the seventh day is a day of rest. Seven because it is a holy number. And Serengeti because his mother was a red Arab who came from the white sands of Africa. Because he was a wonder of the world. Because my father was born in Africa and this horse had something of that wild longing in his soul, to race forever on the land with no barriers.

I brought him home. The trailer rang out with his hooves and swerved as he tried to break the ties that bound him. First thing first, I needed to teach this horse that I was in charge. When we got home, I tied him to a tree. He screamed and reared. He kicked out his back legs. I brought all the children inside and we watched from the window. Seven plunged and reared and screamed for hours, and we all wondered what I had done bringing such a wild horse home.

Little did we realize, he would teach me how to be strong, how to fight, how to submit to God's gentle hand, and most importantly, how to control my emotions. For, without that control, both of us were lost.

After four hours, Seven finally dropped his head. He was covered in sweat. He began to lick his lips, a sign of submission. I untied his lead and walked him to his pen, a large area with grass, fresh water, and plenty of room to run around. For a moment, he put his head to my chest, and I breathed deeply, and then he was off. A vision of beauty and freedom, gold flashing in the evening sun.

We had many adventures, Seven and I. There was much he had to teach me, and God was happy to bring me good friends to help and laugh along the way. A photographer who saw his beauty and, in the process, inspired and taught me photography. True horsewomen, who taught me to stand tall and ask for what was needed. And a vet who gave me the courage to try.

But my dear Seven taught me the most. He inspired me to be strong, to be confident, to be specific in the things I asked for. He taught me how to pray. He taught me how to be obedient to God, for how could I ask the lower creature, a creature so strong and so powerful, to obey me, the weaker creature, if I could not obey God who was superior to me in all ways. He taught me how to trust, for sometimes I asked that horse to trust me when he could only see danger. If he could trust me, a creature that made mistakes, how could I not trust God, who was perfect? And finally, he taught me how to love. For if I could love him, who was wild, imperfect, and impulsive, could I not believe that God loved me infinitely more?

My Seven and I had many rides over hill and dale, alongside the crashing sea, through rivers, and over mountains. The gentle cadence of his lope soothed my anguished soul, the excited clippity-clop of his morning walk lifted my spirits, and the rebellious toss of his head and hinds reminded me to fight for all that is good and beautiful in life. God had provided the perfect companion to heal and strengthen my soul.

And even more important, Seven taught my children how to ride. Yes, that wild creature bowed his fiery head and slowed his quickened walk, so as to keep one, perhaps two, and even three little children on his strong back. He taught them too how to be strong and clear. How to set boundaries and demand what was right. That powerful beast humbled himself before my little children and taught them that the greatest act of strength can sometimes be found in a quiet gentleness of spirit.

FENCES TO BUILD

As we settled into our new home, there were fences to build, horses to ride, and ponds beckoning. We had a wonderland just outside our back door.

But first. The fences. Unless you have built ranch fencing, you have no idea what it takes. First, one must measure out the land to be fenced. In our case, we were fencing and cross-fencing twenty acres. One must plan out not only where each post will be but how far apart they should be and what supporting posts need to be added. A friend of mine came over to our house one day and asked Walt and me what our plan was for fencing. We showed her our proposal. She sat down with us and helped us make a plan for a fence that was "horse-high, pig-tight and bull-strong" and would still be around for our children's children. It required thousands and thousands of dollars, just as many man-hours and some heavy machinery. We may have had the man-hours, but nothing else. She then introduced me to a Nature Conservancy grant as well as her CPA. Between the two, we were able to receive a grant to help with the financing and the CPA managed to bring us massive farm tax breaks. And she, amazingly enough, had the machinery. We looked at the children, now growing into strong men and women, and they could read well enough between the lines. They *were* the man-hours.

There is nothing like building a fence to test the strength of a marriage. Our first step was to walk off the distance. Walter and I held a string and a can of marking spray and proceeded to mark off the place for each fencepost. Except he pulled the string harder than my hold. The string fell to the ground. Cursing. On both sides. "Hold tighter." "Don't pull so hard." And then the discussion of where exactly the fence should go. "In a straight line," said the man. "Around these beautiful bends in the path," said the woman. Glare met glare. The woman won that one, so she held the line tighter as an act of reparation.

Then the placing of posts at each designated spot. This requires a truck, driving in the open range. With large rocks, pits, fallen trees, and not a small amount of cursing from both the man and his wife. They were drowned out, however, by the joyful cries of joy from the kids as they bounced perilously in the back.

And then the wire. Rolls and rolls of wire. The cost was softened by the grant, but the weight was only held by the horse trailer. And so now the horse trailer is bouncing along out back along with the truck. Wife closing her eyes, thankful her man can drive so well. Never mind the truck and trailer parts scattered over fields as the truck and trailer meet tree and rock. The fence was proceeding and that took priority.

How to put a fence post in the ground. Someone must pick up the seven-foot T-post and hold it upright. Then the other person must pick up a *very heavy* T-post pounder. If it is light (and cheap) it will break. We know. Many fell apart, until we found one from the 1800s that weighed probably fifty pounds. So, now person No. 2 must pick this up, and place it on top of the T-post. Person No. 1 must worry considerably about person No. 2 dropping the pounder or missing the T-post altogether and be ready to move quickly out of the way. Once the T-post pounder is on top of the T-post, the pounder must be lifted and dropped or pounded on the post. That this can be done over and over without injury is somewhat of a miracle of engineering and strength.

Folks have asked why my children are so uncommonly strong. Everything they need to know is right there in those posts.

But the best part of a long day working on fencing is when it's time for refreshment in the beautiful clear ponds. At a certain point, Mom sees the flagging spirits and worn backs, and she declares the day's work to be over. Everyone heads for the ponds and creeks and jumps in. Boys are shirtless, girls in their tank tops, everyone wet and cool and happy. Even Mom, who has done a smidgen of the work but mostly directs, frolics in the cool spring.

In sum, I will add that there is nothing better than building a fence to teach a child hard work, honesty, and perseverance. The ground does not care a bit what you say to it, how much you mouth off, how tired you are, or how much you disagree. It needs to be pounded and mastered all the same. A well-placed T-post is a thing of pride, and at the day's end, you can see your work, know it's well done, and sleep well. I highly recommend miles and miles of fencing for the raising of children and teaching of natural virtues.

THE SURGEON

"Let us understand that God is a physician, and that suffering is a medicine for salvation, not a punishment for damnation" —St. Augustine.

The following years were good years. We raised animals, sheep, goats, pigs, steers, chickens, ducks, and puppies. We put in an orchard and a garden, we enjoyed the creeks and riding the horses. Boys boycotted the horses and bought quads and plenty of fun was had with these as well. Every year we had a "Top Shot" competition wherein we took every weapon we could find—all the guns, knives, arrows, javelins, paintball guns, and even rocks—and had a daylong competition of who could be the most accurate.

We played soccer, baseball, football, and Frisbee. Franz helped us put in a competition-size volleyball court, with three layers of sand. We played hard, ate off the land, and laughed and talked.

During this time of peace and prosperity, our sweet Lord worked within my heart. Teaching me lessons and purifying my soul. He knew best my weaknesses and knew best how to cure them. He would bring me sorrow, and I would call my sister. Heidi is my greatest critic and greatest fan. And I pride myself on the returning of both favors. She too would call me with sorrow. And we both were quite happy to point out the flaw in each other that was being corrected. As well, we consoled and loved and cried with each other.

So, we learned that with every cross came healing. With every sorrow, a salve. The surgeon was precise in his cuts, even if they hurt.

He called me to His most loving heart, and in my pain and sorrow, I was comforted. When Satan attacked me with fear, I prayed the rosary. "I believe in God, the Father Almighty, Creator of heaven and earth." Over and over as my heart beat with panic. God. Father. Creator. What had I to fear? And as I prayed, I breathed. As I breathed, I prayed more and asked our Lord. "What would you have me do?" And with each breath, I had an understanding of my trouble and then an understanding of how to get out of my trouble. Satan causes panic, our Lord has the answers. And so, I learned, with every panic attack, how to trust in God. How to go to Him in times of trouble. And most importantly, that with any problem, no matter how big, He was there with an answer.

As the years went by, I began to trust our Lord and knew that He had made me from the first moment in the womb, cowardly and weak as I was, and that He would never ask more of me than I was able to give. And most of all, every joy, every sorrow was either for the salvation of my soul or the salvation of others. And He, being a generous and loving Father, gave me the grace to see it.

***

COVID'S JOY

And then…COVID. Shut down. Fourteen days to stop the spread.

One after another, schools were closed and children sent home. The table was first cleared of projects and then pushed out from the wall to make more room. Chairs were brought from every corner of the house and hustled next to one another, fitting another and yet another until there was no more space. Suddenly our calm, charming dinner was transformed into a lively and animated event filled with ideas, debate, and mirth. The house was full, yes. Very full. Every couch claimed, every carpet space claimed, every corner full of backpacks and books, and every table full of Chromebooks, laptops, and cellphones. But oh! That house was full of happiness! We played every sort of game, had adventures galore, played in the creek, took hikes, rode the horses, rode the quads, played volleyball, played soccer, and Frisbee. We made a chart, and everyone happily took turns cooking and cleaning.

William and Karl adored their older brothers and loved having them home to play their wild games and adventures. This gift of brotherhood was precious. We enjoyed this extended vacation with nothing to do and nowhere to go, and especially in our beautiful Mariposa spring. We had five going horseback-riding, girls had a baking competition, and boys had a cooking competition. At night we played canasta or bridge, with two tables going at the same time, we watched movies or shared conversations. Laughter and play were our constant companions that spring. Every bed and couch was filled, every chair was taken, every plate was full, and every face a smile.... And the washing machine never stopped.

In the middle of it all, my dear friend and priest says to me: "Enjoy this. It will not last." He had no idea. But surely God did.

PREPARATION FOR SORROWS

Finally, the schools opened up and everyone packed their bags and went back to school. Once again, our home was quiet with just William, Karl, Walter, and me. A different season.

During this time of quiet, I was at Mass, and was inspired to pray:

"Lord, I give myself entirely to you. Fill me with your love. Everything that is good in me is from you. Everything weak and afraid is from me."

He responded, "Even if that brings suffering?"

"Lord, where else would I go?"

As I received Him in Communion, I had an image in my heart of our Lord on the cross. He was embracing me, and my heart was bleeding. His heart was bleeding, and our blood was blended together. He had his arms around me, and I knew that any suffering I had would be joined to him. In that suffering, I would be embraced by Him.

My son Franz. With bright blue eyes and golden hair. Who smiled and charmed his mother with his ready laugh and charming wit. Franz, who was a godly son. Who helped everyone he met. Franz, who could carve wood to look like anything he imagined. He once created a worn and much-loved baseball out of the hardest wood around us, the beautiful red manzanita. He received top grades at Thomas Aquinas College and then earned a coveted Navy Scholarship to become a dentist—one out of four in the nation to receive that honor. Franz was one of the strongest and most fit in multiple Spartan Race competition. He went to dental school and again was top of the class. My son who came home for the holidays and loved nothing more than celebrating his brothers' and sisters' weddings and their forthcoming children. That son was made for a special sacrifice. I just did not know. I simply loved him.

I became sick. A strange sickness that caused me terrible pain, high fevers, and exhaustion. I was tested for COVID. It was not COVID. I had over 250 blood tests taken and none of them was positive. Still, I lingered. In pain and exhaustion. I prayed and offered my suffering to God. I could not focus on a single intention because my head hurt so bad. More tests. More shaking of head. For twenty-one days. Seven days times three. Holy numbers. It was a novena, and I knew it. I prayed and prayed. My body was being purified.

I could not eat. Only drink. It was a fast; unbidden and unwelcome. On November 25, twenty-one days later, my fever broke. Just in time to prepare for Thanksgiving. We had a lovely day of celebration. A few days of family joy. A respite before the cross. A last supper before the Garden. I did not know. I simply loved.

CHAPTER 7

Franz

✦

THE PHONE CALL

Thanksgiving was simple. Just us four, Walter, William, Karl and me. Everyone was busy. Living different lives. I consoled myself with the fact they were all coming home for Christmas. "One month," I thought, "and we will all be together again." It was Saturday after Thanksgiving; the sun was warm through the window and the house clean and tranquil. Walter was off at the office preparing for trial, and I sat at the kitchen table surrounded by receipts, starting my taxes. It was a quiet time to review my year, a time of praise and thanksgiving.

The phone rings.

I pick it up and hear a choked voice that sounds far away. "Mrs. Wall. I am so sorry to call you. There has been an accident. Franz is hurt." I hear tears. Choking. "I am so sorry to be the one to tell you this. We were skiing and he went off a jump. I think he is paralyzed."

I stand with the phone in my hand, frozen. If I can't feel, horror can't find me. If I am still enough, it will pass by. I ask quietly "Where is he now?" "He is at the ICU in

Reno, Nevada. I am so sorry. So sorry, Mrs. Wall. This is my phone number."

The room is spinning. I think I hung up on him. There are scrawls on an envelope, which are an attempt at writing down the friend's phone number and the name of the hospital. I don't know what to do. I have a photo shoot in an hour, do I cancel? With COVID, will they even let me in the hospital? Nevada!? How far away is that? What do I do? I try and call the hospital and get an automated recording with so many choices. I want to scream, "Where is my son!?"

I call Walter. He says words that I do not understand, and I hang up. I call the hospital and finally find a human. They don't have a patient named Franz Wall. How bad could this be? Should I drive to Nevada? I am wandering around the house mumbling and bumping into things. Bernadette is home and calls her dad. "Something happened. Mom isn't making sense. I don't know what to do."

Walter calls me again and tells me "You have to go to Franz." A clear instruction. "Take Bernadette." And then he tells Bernadette. "Take care of your mom. Make sure she packs clothes. Make sure she puts gas in the tank. Make sure she eats and drinks water."

I stuff some underwear in a bag and think: "I need a jacket. Franz was skiing. He must be cold." I plan to be gone one night. One night. I had no idea of the nightmare that was unfolding before us.

It is a long drive, over the mountains full of snow. Through the mountains that hurt my boy. Over the Donner Pass where Satan ate humans. My thoughts are wild and out of control. I try and focus on the road. As we drive, I call Franz's friend and try to get more information on how to contact the hospital. Finally, I am able to confirm the address of the hospital and confirm there is a patient, Franz Wall. He is being seen in the ER. Only one visitor the entire visit. I tell his friend: "Do not go in. Do not see him. I am that person." He is doing everything to be helpful. Kind. Apologetic. He waits for us at the hospital. We drive. My headache is so severe, I can barely see. I am driving nearly blind with fear and worry. Bernadette makes me pull over to drink water, fill up on gas and go pee. I force myself to breathe.

Suddenly the phone rings. I see Franz's picture. I am so excited that I have to pull off the road so as not to crash. For a moment, I think it is all a mistake. That I will hear Franz's booming voice telling me he is just fine. I plan to laugh in joy and scold him lovingly. Such desperate lonely thoughts.

But it is the nurse. "Franz has been injured very badly. He is paralyzed and cannot move from the chest down. He cannot use his hands. He is about to go into surgery. They are going to put in a spinal cradle to stabilize his neck and hopefully reduce swelling. It is a dangerous surgery and I thought you would want to talk to him before he goes in." Her kindness hurts my heart because she knows more than I do. She finishes with "Do you want to talk to him?"

"cannot use his hands…"

"surgery to stabilize his neck…"

I nearly scream "Yes!" to her question.

"cannot use his hands…" Those words creep like ice-cold tendrils of horror in my mind.

I hear Franz's voice, "Mom."

"Oh, my son! My son!" My heart splits open, there on the side of the road. What do I say? What is the single most important thing to say before he goes into surgery, where I may lose him forever? In that moment in time, I think only two things. The most important and necessary things he needs to know. The muscle memory of so many crosses, so many prayers, so many trials, and so many blessings. God has prepared me for this exact moment in time, and I am wrapped in fierce conviction.

"Franz, I love you."

"I love you, Mom. I think I'm paralyzed."

"Franz you are going to be OK. Do you hear me? God has given this to you for your salvation and the salvation of souls."

"I know, Mom." He says with absolute clarity and conviction. "And it is the most important thing."

"Goodbye Mom. I love you."

And it was the last thing I heard him say for a very long time.

THE ICU

Bernadette and I arrive at the hospital in Reno and park. We wander into a part of the parking garage set aside for COVID victims. It is a huge cement room full of beds, each cordoned off with plastic. It looks more like a graveyard for the living than anything else. We shudder. Death seems like a cold ghost wrapping around my soul.

We finally find the entrance and make it past the guard who has to take our temperature. I am shivering with shock by now and manage to say through rattling teeth that I am here to see my son in the ER. I tell him he was in a ski accident. The guard looks at me with sad eyes and says: "I heard that one come in. Emergency heli-flight. We thought he was going to die."

I am sick and can barely stand. Bernadette holds me up. Franz's friend comes to me with kind, sorrowful eyes. Tears flutter on my eyelashes and all my silly thoughts that I can "handle this" evaporate. I feel small and helpless.

I ask for directions to the ICU and leave Bernadette at the entrance of the hospital with Franz's friend, who awkwardly stays by her side. He doesn't want to leave her alone but doesn't know what to do. I don't think of it at the time, but he's been there all day, worried and sick about his friend.

I arrive at the waiting room of the ICU and announce my name on the intercom. I am told someone will come out. A woman sits with me and tells me cheerfully, "This is my day forty-two."

I am stunned. "*Forty-two days*? What is she talking about? I am planning on going home tomorrow." She tells me how her boyfriend was in a motorcycle accident forty-two days ago and was paralyzed. She stayed for a month and then had to go home and work. Now she visits every Saturday. She explains, "He still can't speak, and I spend our time trying to figure out what he says to me." She paused a moment, looking sad. "Sometimes, I spend all day figuring out letters and then what he says doesn't make sense." I simply stare at her and attempt to smile, but inside I am crumbling. What is happening? Whose life am I in? Won't Franz just walk away with bounding muscles and his big old grin? Won't a motherly pep talk solve all the problems? ...Forty-two days?

I can't remember if I prayed. I just focused on not fainting. I think death must be like this. "At the hour of my death..." Mary watch over me. Lord, lead me out of temptation. Guardian angel guide me. For sometimes, when our hearts and minds are paralyzed, it is only the habit of prayer and the memory of faith that sustains us.

Finally, the nurse comes out and talks to me. She is disturbingly kind. Franz is coming out of surgery. He is doing well. The doctor will talk to me in an hour. I think about Bernadette stuck at the entrance of the hospital. I tell the nurse that I will be back and make my way through the long halls, asking for directions, lost, confused, my mind in a cloud of shock, and finally find Bernadette. Franz's friend is standing there awkwardly, and Bernadette smiles a strained smile. He gives me a hug, and I thank him and say something awkward like it was delightful to meet him though I wished it was in better times.

He asks if I want to get Franz's things. A jolt of sickness washes through me. "His things." As if he was dead. The things he had before everything changed. His thick blanket that we gave him as a boy. His backpack full of schoolwork. His wallet full of money, ready for an exciting adventure. All the things he had packed and used, never knowing this would happen. I take his things and put them in my truck. We say goodbye, and Bernadette and I check into the hotel that is connected to the hospital. I pay for one night. It is still beyond my comprehension that I will not be leaving with Franz tomorrow. I have no idea that I will spend the next thirty days in this hospital, willing my son to live.

We check in and I go back to the waiting room outside the ICU. Finally, I am called in. I am taken to "the room." That horrible room you always see that is meant to give family the really bad news. I always wondered what it was like to sit there, knowing your life was collapsing.

And here I sit, waiting for the doctor. He comes in like a force of nature. Shocking white hair, six foot eight inches tall, a broad, expressive face, and looking, for all the world, like a Titan god. He shows me X-rays of my son's neck and explains. "Look, your son has a C-5, C-6 injury. We can't tell much, but it looks complete. He won't walk or use his hands. He will have limited use of his arms. Maybe won't be able to breathe on his own. The biggest problem we have is swelling, which will cut off more capabilities. I put in a brace to help with that. Any questions?" I grow faint and the room dims and blurs. "Can I see him?"

They take me back to see my son. I will never forget that moment. My son, bound with muscles and strength, my son whose hands can create such beauty, my son with his charming smile and blinding wit. He lays now on a hospital bed tied down, unable to breathe, unable to walk. My heart catches in my throat and tears come unbidden from my eyes.

He sees me and cries out to me. His face full of fear, sorrow, and sadness. He flexes his arms but they are tied to the bed. Tears fall down his cheeks and he reaches out to me, like a child looking for his mama's comfort. I run to him and hold him. My big strong son. I remember when he was a baby and hurt himself, but I cannot kiss this hurt away. No, not this one. The impossibility of his injury overwhelms me. I caress his forehead and hold the arms that want to wrap around me in grief. I am at a loss as to how to comfort him. So I sing, oh so softly, the songs I sang to him as a baby. He weeps and my heart is breaking in ways I cannot describe. I tell him he must sleep so he can get better. I put my head close to his face and kiss his cheek. Tears fall down his face and mingle with mine.

PRAYING FOR A MIRACLE

Nothing, nothing could have prepared me for such destruction and such grief. I could not stand, and the nurses brought me a chair. It was only my desire to comfort my son that I did not faint. His muscle-bound legs were pinned to a brace that pulled them to the end of the bed. His powerful chest and lungs were filled with air from a machine. His arms were tied to the bed like a captive. I would have died for love of him if it would have helped.

The nurse explained to me that his legs had blown eight inches out of their sockets. He had a punctured lung. He was not breathing well on his own. He was fighting the tracheotomy, so his hands had to be tied down. He was paralyzed. He would not be able to use his hands. No wood carving. No dentistry. No volleyball or soccer or Frisbee. No building things for his mama. All of that is gone. In a moment. The nurse reminded me that his brain was intact and had not been damaged. At least that. A glimmer of something left of my son. I did not realize how long it would be to see that glimmer.

As I walked back to the hotel, I made a quiet prayer about putting this heartbreak on Facebook. We were in the middle of a terrible political division, and many did not trust FB, had left FB, and were no longer communicating with friends. Without knowing the reason, I felt compelled to tell Franz's story and to beg for prayers. So, I put out a post:

I feel like I'm in some horrible nightmare that I can't wake up from. Franz was in a terrible ski accident and is paralyzed from the chest down.

My son's hands are tied down. There are bolts in his legs attached to weights. He is suffocating and cannot breathe. He looks at his mother with absolute love and I return the look of love—willing to absorb his pain. I stand at the foot of my son's cross and ask the angels to hold me up. I can feel every beat of my heart and my head hasn't stopped pounding. I unite my sorrows to Our Lady, Christ's mother, and ask for her help. I ask her to wrap me in her mantle. For she saw the miracle in her son's death and I too pray for a miracle, but in my son's life.

His father is sitting at the kitchen table, crying. The children at home are lost and confused. No one knows what to do.

I have only my faith and conviction that somehow this is all in God's hands and He allowed this for a greater good. Though for me, I see nothing. I suppose that is why we call it faith.

Please pray for our son.

THE CHURCH MILITANT

By the time I got back to our hotel room, I was worn to the core of my soul and realized I had not eaten all day. I was too exhausted to figure out what to do but knew I needed to do something. As I walked in the door, I saw, on the dresser, a feast spread out before me. Bernadette stood beside it, smiling a huge smile.

I gasped in astonishment. "What angel brought this food?" I asked.

"I don't know, Mom. Someone just came to the hotel room with all this food. Someone saw your post and they knew someone else in Reno. They told me someone would come every night that we were here. And, Mom, look at all this!"

And what she showed me took my breath away. Dinners had been arranged for Bernadette and me at the hotel, as well as for my kids at home. Many offered to help with daily care of the ranch. My small Facebook post asking for prayers for my son had exploded and gone all over the continent. It was shared over and over. To convents. To monasteries. To schoolrooms of little children. To prayer groups in every state. To the California Dental Association, to the Navy Moms, to Thomas Aquinas College, Wyoming Catholic College, and so many other colleges. Facebook became flooded with images of "Pray for Franz." His cousin set up a GoFundMe account, which was increasing by the moment. The dental office that had hired Franz before dental school and had taught him the state-of-the-art advancements in dental work had made a bold donation to the GoFundMe page. Even more profoundly, they promised to help bring him back into dentistry when he returned, not only bringing hope but reminding him of their friendship and their faith in him.

My friend arranged the infamous "Taco Tuesday" for donations from a local taco truck and arranged anonymous donations to cover hotel and food costs. "Fight4Franz" shirts were generated by friends and put out for sale, all proceeds to Franz. Angels in our midst. I was overwhelmed.

One Facebook post read: "Who is this guy? He is blowing up my Facebook feed!" Within moments, he was flooded with answers and stories of Franz's kindness. He finally said, "Well, add in my prayers—he must be one hell of a kid!" My mother's heart was overwhelmed, I had not known of Franz's accomplishments and kindness. He was just the kid doing what he loved and bringing everyone along with him.

And the best of all, the men in Mariposa got together and decided that Walter needed to be with me, even if he couldn't see his son. And so, they arranged everything, including a friend, flying Walter in a private plane to Reno. When Walter arrived, I fell into his arms. I was beyond grateful to have him with me.

That night, the hospital made an exception and let Walter visit. Walter went to see his son. The enormity of the damage hit him, and he broke down crying over his son. Franz was shaking and emotional. It was harder to watch both my men breaking down. I comforted both, and then the father spoke so lovingly and with such strength and you could see it transfer to his son. The miracle of a man and his boy.

Walter finally returned to our room. His face was washed gray with grief. A second beautiful bounty was spread before us, but Walter could barely eat. The look between us said it all. Love. Sorrow. Faith. For in the midst of all this, we both knew. We knew. God is good and is walking with us. But even so, our sorrow was consuming.

That night, I awoke sometime before dawn. The night was dark. But the dawn was just whispering, dispelling the darkness. The sky was dusted with a soft blue and pink. The merest suggestion of light. The promise of the day. The last stars gave off their light, almost laughing at the darkness because it cannot take away their shine.

And in that moment, I had a vision.

Walt and I are in a deep valley. It is dark and there is a monster in that valley. In the dark and fog, we only see it in glimpses. A long, dangerous tail. Red, bloodthirsty eyes. Long, vicious teeth, soiled with the flesh it has consumed and destroyed. It circles us, coiling and roaring its fire. Walt and I stand against it, hand in hand, our hearts beating in our chests. Our children stand behind us, for it is not only our worn and scarred souls it wants, but our sweet, beautiful children. Our children stand with their spouses. And their families stand with them. And our grandchildren, vulnerable but also a powerful testament of sacramental love. Purity and goodness. The monster hates that profession of love, right there in our little family. He hates our bigger extended family, standing against Satan.

But this monster is terrible. We tremble in fear, despair curling around our hearts like a poisonous fog.

And then they come. The soldiers. The prayer warriors. The friends. The ones who barely know us, who have only heard of us. "Half of Texas is praying for you." "Mariposa strong." All over the world, I receive messages. I am in tears with the generosity. Those who have never said a prayer in their life, joining this army in their first prayer. Those who are seasoned warriors, who fast and make sacrifices. Mothers who offer up the demands of their children, fathers going to work every day. Friends. Family. The immense Body of Christ. Standing there against Satan. Calling upon their Lord and Savior. An overwhelming swelling of prayers fills the air and surrounds the canyon with light. The dark valley barely contains the love of this great army. Their prayers echo and shake the earth with their force.

And He is there. The almighty and most powerful God. He stands against Satan, and before Him, Satan retreats. He has no fight here. And so, he crawls away, sucking with himself all the fear, hatred, and despair. And Love stands. A massive, mighty force of good. The Church Militant.

But there is a deeper truth. And this was the truth that I wrestled with. God has victory over death. If Franz had died, my heart would have broken and truly I might have died from that broken heart. But that monster would not have won. No, heaven would have gained a beautiful soul. For, Franz was ready to be with our Lord.

In the Triumph of the Cross, God won final victory over death. For we know: "O death, where is thy sting? O grave, where is thy victory? The sting of death is sin....But thanks be to God, which giveth us victory through our Lord Jesus Christ" (1 Corinthians 15:55-57).

God allowed Franz to live another day. To do more good upon this earth. And for that, I thank Him and praise Him. But the greater truth is that while each of us must succumb to death, God's victory is a life of eternity in heaven.

As the days went by, the testimonies followed. So many stories of love and encouragement. Stories of how Franz had helped or inspired them. Stories of kindness and laughter. Offers of help, books to read, treasures sent. Rosaries prayed.

But also, there were stories of those who had been lost and were coming back to Christ. Of those who had walked into a church for the first time in twenty years. Stories from those who did not know the words but were searching for Christ.

While our son struggled to breathe, we were witnessing a miracle of faith. The Church Militant had gone to war on behalf of our son and by that battle, souls were being saved. We were deeply humbled, grateful, and in awe of the power of God.

OUR LADY'S FOOTSTEPS

Day 4: *My heart is heavy, sad, and tired. I am such a weak soul, already worn down by tribulation and bravery. Franz has a high fever and pneumonia. It is very dangerous and damaging his lungs. Franz tries to talk to us, but he cannot. His face is twisted in agony because he has a tube down his throat. Tears fill his eyes and come down each cheek. He reaches out to hug me, but his arms are still tied to the bed. Those great strong arms. There is nothing that can be done. I look at him, willing to absorb his pain. My body cannot contain my grief. I hold his hand and he realizes he cannot feel my hand. We are both at a loss. He shakes his head and closes his eyes. It is breaking my heart that I don't know how to help him. I don't know how to help him carry his cross.*

We found a daily Mass. It was a Spanish Mass of very devout men and women. Their prayers were like a beautiful song, flowing over us. I sat in their presence and let their prayers wash over me. I let their prayers speak for me because I had no words, just a blind, blind faith. I gave myself to Our Lord, gave myself to Him as a servant. "Lord, I am not worthy... But only say the word..." I looked up at the beautiful, horrible crucifix. Christ, bloody, on the cross.

Suddenly, I see those twisted legs, tied down so brutally. The arms spread out and also tied. The look of anguish. The lungs that are suffocating. My heart catches. It is my Franz. There on the cross. I cannot stop the flood of tears. I think about Mary and how she would have died of sorrow if angels had not held her up. I know, then, that angels are holding me up. I think about Mary as Christ carries His cross. She cannot hold Him. Cannot kiss his torn knees when He falls.

She has no words to give Him. And she cannot carry His cross. She can only look on with love and hope it brings comfort. I am helpless. And yet, I am comforted by the company I have found. For what greater mother than the mother of our Lord? I am deeply thankful that I have seen Christ in Franz. Grateful for the tied arms and legs. Grateful for the sorrow. Because I perceive dimly that in walking with Our Lady, I have been given a great gift.

ALL THE KING'S MEN

A mighty force had gathered on behalf of Franz. We received calls from the University of the Pacific Dental School. They told me in tears as well as tones of awe, how amazing Franz was. How he had helped each of his classmates to succeed. How well-loved he was and how he inspired the teachers. I was overwhelmed. As with many parents of adult children, they go off into the world and you pray and hope for the best. He sent texts that he was doing well, but we did not know he was at the top of his class. He sent pictures of parties and fun times, but we did not know he was chosen by his classmates to represent the school with the California Dental Association as well as the Dental Insurance Company. We knew he had won a very competitive scholarship with the navy that paid for dental school, but we did not know what the navy thought of him, if it even cared, if it even knew he existed.

Within the first week, the school called me to tell me Franz had signed up for insurance and that it covered 80 percent. I had no idea his first month in the hospital would cost over a million dollars. We were told Franz needed rehabilitation when he came home and that it would take an ambulance to transport him. The gravity of his situation began to sink in. Rehabilitation? An ambulance? You mean we weren't going to throw him in the truck and bring him home?

We were referred to a rehabilitation facility. Holding the number in our hands, Walter and I sat in our truck under the cold Nevada sky. We sat and shivered even though the heater was on. Holding our breath and gathering our courage, we called. She told us: "Franz will be here for a few weeks, and in the meantime, you need to put in a handicap bathroom, ramp, and do you have a full-time nurse to take care of him? Are you medically trained to care for his needs?" We began to shake. I opened the car door and threw up. We looked at each other and thought the same thing: "Our son. Our son. What has happened to our strong, powerful, capable son? How can we possibly manage all this?"

We drove back to the hotel, whatever errands we had in mind had long ago evaporated. I crawled into bed and shook with grief. Walter sat next to me, holding me, his own tears falling upon my face.

Poor Bernadette had to sit in that room, trying to study, earphones in place. Trying to drown out her parents' sorrow as well as her own.

And then we received a phone call. It was from the navy. He introduced himself as a doctor from the navy who was in charge of Franz's scholarship. I did not know who he was or how he knew us. His call arrived like an angel's greeting. "I am Dr. M. Your son is an incredible young man, and we are going to do everything we can to help him. Do you realize that his accident occurred while he was in active-duty status? Because of this, he has very good insurance with the navy, which will cover all his expenses. I am contacting everyone that needs to be contacted. How are you doing, ma'am? Can I help you with anything?"

Overwhelmed, I manage to say: "We need to pay for a rehabilitation facility, and we need to retrofit our home. Those are my biggest worries. Other than my son. Who cannot walk."

"I will start working on that right away, ma'am. And my deepest condolences for your son. He is an incredible young man. I wish I could fix him."

DEMONS AND ANGELS

Day 6: *Last night I had a terrible dream. I dreamt there was a demon. I crushed it beneath my foot and then took a razor blade and aggressively cut off its head. It was a long process, and I did it with clenched teeth. For what mama bear would not savagely rip the living hell out of anyone that hurt her child?*

But the waters became bloody with this demon's blood. And soon its arms reached through the contaminated water and then its vicious grinning face. Still alive and determined to destroy. I cried out in my sleep, and Walter, my faithful protector, woke me up and knew. He began a rosary asking for Mary's protection over his wife. I rested in his arms and prayed with him. I pondered the meaning of the dream.

I realized that evil cannot be met with evil. It can only be conquered with faith, hope, and love. Please pray for me. Between the hours of two and five, the demons haunt me. They torture me with fear and laugh at my pain. I know I am engaged in a terrible battle. With so many good souls praying, they are furious and want to destroy me. I am painfully aware our room is not blessed, and we have no crucifix.

Within hours of this post, a crusade was mobilized. A prayer petition was sent out from friends to convents and schools, to mothers' groups and colleges. I could not believe my eyes when a prayer calendar was sent to me stating who would pray for me on what day and at what hour. All so that I would know someone was praying for me as I struggled with the demons of fear and despair.

Then the gifts arrived. We were brought to tears as holy water arrived, a crucifix, and rosaries. Someone came to the apartment with a statue of Our Lady of Guadalupe. How could they have known?

And then I received a message with a box. I recognized the name. "This is from my parents who both passed away. We found it in their home, and we know it was very precious to them. It is special water from a rock. Maybe in Italy. It is called Lourdes water. Do you know it? Maybe it was blessed by a priest? Please pray for us. We are baptized Catholic and have never been interested in any faith, but we are so greatly inspired by yours and are deeply moved. Please accept this gift."

This gift perhaps meant more than any of the others because a soul was awakening and feeling the warmth of faith and God's love. There is no greater treasure than a soul who has come back to Christ.

"So, he told them this parable: 'What man of you, having a hundred sheep, if he has lost one of them, does not leave the ninety-nine in the open country, and go after the one that is lost, until he finds it? And when he has found it, he lays it on his shoulders, rejoicing. And when he comes home, he calls together his friends and his neighbors, saying to them, "Rejoice with me, for I have found my sheep that was lost." Just so, I tell you, there will be more joy in heaven over one

sinner who repents than over ninety-nine righteous persons who need no repentance'" (Luke 15:3-7).

A man texted me and told me about his son who had a terrible accident. He told me of how horrible the ICU was, and how much his son struggled. I was overwhelmed with gratitude that someone else understood the hell I was living in. One sleepless night, I texted him at three in the morning. I figured he could respond later in the day. But he texted me back right away. "I understand," he said. "It will get better." I just sat in the bathroom, shivering. He was a lifeline of hope. Another mother whose daughter had a terrible accident texted me. She said: "I am always here. I know. I KNOW." These were only some of my lifelines of hope. And yet, sometimes, it was just me, laying in my husband's arms, sobbing my grief, while Bernadette lay in her bed, in the corner of the room listening to her parent's cry, feeling like she had become the adult and not knowing what to do.

I was so overwhelmed by the kindness and generosity of those friends, family, and strangers who circled us with love. I thought about those who do not have so much support and prayed for them. I prayed for their souls and for their courage.

I asked myself, "What kind of spiritual battle is this, that so many are needed as soldiers?"

It seemed that it was not simply for the physical healing of my son's paralysis, it must also be for the salvation of his soul. And he, a good boy, who followed the commandments, who was kind and loving to those around him, what kind of peril was he in? Why was Satan so interested in his soul that God brought thousands to fight for him? I became dimly aware that we cannot see the spiritual danger we face and that God protects us from. We go through life laughing, eating, drinking, sleeping, and praying, never realizing that we walk the edge of life and death, heaven and hell. We presume our safety. And perhaps that is the point. Because the fact of the matter is that God provides for us with an abundance of generosity that we cannot even see.

CHAPTER 8

The Perfect Joy of Suffering

THE PRIVILEGE

Day 8: *"Blessed are all who wait for the Lord. He heals the brokenhearted and binds up their wounds."*

I go to my afternoon visit. My slow shuffle to sorrow. My time to prepare myself, to reflect on what my son might need from me. My long walk down many halls that are only slightly familiar because I am so internally reflective that I notice little.

I arrive at the ICU, out of breath from emotional exhaustion. I take a deep breath, square my shoulders, and announce my name. With a buzz, I am in the inner sanctum.

The nurse comes to me and tells me that Franz stopped breathing last night. His lungs just quit taking oxygen. They had to massage them. I don't know what that means. They are giving him medicine so that his lungs are soft, and they absorb oxygen. She tells me, "Franz is very sick." And I understand that he may not survive.

When I heard this, I just collapse. Sobbing, holding his hand, praying the rosary. Great, gasping sobs of helplessness, grief. Sobbing because there is a God and I need him. Franz can't fix himself. I can't fix him. Only God can fix him, and He may not. He may choose not to fix Franz. Franz is totally and completely in the hands of God, and I am powerless. Wracking sobs that tear the body in half and wrench the soul into shreds.

The nurse comes in and I wipe my face, trying to compose myself. It is time for Franz to exercise. He starts off willing enough: shoulders, arms, and then tried to use his hands. My mother's heart will never forget the look of horror when my twenty-six-year-old son, who loves to carve, to make teeth, to build porches, and to hold babies, when that man realizes he cannot move his hands. The anguish on his face tears my heart in two, and I don't know if I will ever recover. Tears stream down his face. I hug him and kiss him and tell him he must keep working on it. Break it down into baby steps. He resolves again and keeps trying. I try to be strong and encourage him.

But then he gestures, and I can't understand. I ask him, do you want this? Or this? And the nurse says he wants to write. My poor boy doesn't realize he can't write. He has been writing for twenty years and he cannot imagine what it means not to write. Nurse holds up a paper with the alphabet—this letter. This *row? He lifts his hand to point, but he cannot point. Just stubborn blocks of flesh on the end of his arm. Tears stream down his face, and he becomes more and more agitated. He opens his arms and I ask if he wants a hug and tears stream down his face as he nods. Our tears mingle as we hug. Then I ask him if he wants me to go and he nods. The pain is too much for both of us to bear. I hug him again and leave. My heart is all over that bed in so many pieces, I don't know how it will ever be repaired.*

Today at Mass were beautiful readings about hope and healing. But behind the altar was a painting of Abraham and Isaac. Remember Abraham had been promised, as a very old man with a very old wife, that his descendants would be as numerous as the stars. Isaac was born to them. Their only son. And then God asked Abraham to sacrifice Isaac. Abraham took his son to the altar, built a fire, and lifted the knife. An angel stopped him and brought a lamb—truly a foreshadowing of God sacrificing Christ, the perfect lamb. I thought how much we must each be willing to give everything to God, should He ask. I thought how heartbroken Abraham must have been and how frightened Isaac must have been. But the son was spared because Christ offered himself as the perfect victim.

And somehow, somehow, I must have the faith of Abraham and be at peace with whatever God decides to do with my son. Somehow, I must not die of heartache.

*I do not know where to turn. My mind is
black. I trust in God, trust in His most holy will.
I cling to Our Lady of Sorrows. I am being held
up by your faith, your prayers, your love. I myself
am empty and cling to my raft of faith as storms
toss me without resistance.*

After this visit, I called my dear friend and priest. "I do
not understand," I said. "Why am I being given so much
sorrow?" His answer seeped into my broken soul and
began to change my life. He said: "You are being given the
special privilege of walking with Mary on her Via Delarosa.
You are being given the incredible privilege of sharing in
Mary's sorrow of watching her Son tortured and crucified
for your sins and the salvation of souls. Do not be afraid.
Unite yourself with Mary. Offer your heartache with Mary
for the salvation of souls."

I was moved to the depths of my soul. I knew that he
was right. I was filled with gratitude that I have been asked
to share with Our Lady her sorrow over her Son. What a
humbling gift that I could share with Our Lady, the greatest love a woman can carry. What a great gift to enter into
that private and sacred life of our Blessed Mother at the
crucifixion of her Son, our God. I was so in awe of this gift
that I was happy for the piercing of my heart and would not
wish it away for the world.

WALKING IN LENT

Day 9: *Morning Update:*
Second Sunday of Advent
Today's Reading:

Go up onto a high mountain,
Zion, herald of glad tidings.
Cry out at the top of your voice,
Jerusalem, herald of good news!
Fear not to cry out
and say to the cities of Judah:
Here is your God!

After last night, which was rough, I was dreading calling the hospital. Dreading. I called, got put on hold, and thought I may just die of a heart attack.

Nurse comes on: "Hello Miss Christy. Franz had a peaceful night. His oxygen levels are beautiful!"

I have to sit down as relief washes over me. Hope surges through my heart and body like a rushing wind. No—a mighty storm!

Day 9: *Evening Update:*
Herein lies our daily prayer, "Heal Franz in body and in soul." Because we would not forgo the soul for the body. First Lord, purify our son so that he

may live with you forever; second, bring healing to his body. Soul first, body second.

Today, my blessed boy made a sign of the cross. A clumsy one, just like when he was a little boy, showing his mama he could pray. The priest came in and said he was going to pray; did he want Latin or English? Franz clearly mouthed "Latin." So, Latin it was. The priest prayed and Franz mouthed the words he knew. The priest laid his hands on Franz and prayed for complete healing of body and soul. Like the man in the gospel.

Then the priest offered to say the rosary. Franz nodded. "Which mystery? Joyful?" No movement. "Sorrowful?" Nod. A sword piercing my heart. We said the Sorrowful mysteries. The Agony in the Garden. The Scourging. The Crowning of Thorns. The Carrying of the Cross. The Crucifixion. I knew my boy was deep in reflection, contemplating his sufferings alongside those of Christ. He could not move his fingers across the beads, so just like when he was a little boy and I taught him to say the rosary, I helped him with his beads. He gave me such a profound look of deep love, my voice caught, and a tear escaped my mother's eyes.

Afterward, the priest said, "This is a very special rosary, I will give it to you if you promise to pray for me." Franz nodded weakly, but that was not good enough. "No, Franz, this came from Lourdes! It is very special, and you must promise to pray for me." Franz opened his eyes, looked directly at the priest, and nodded.

Franz then received the tiniest piece of communion and just smiled. The most beautiful, content smile I have seen. This moment, of all the moments, is the only one Franz remembers from his time in the ICU.

Patience, Mama. Patience. We are privileged to walk this journey in Advent, a time of great hope, the heavens and earth anticipating the arrival of Christ, the coming of salvation. This journey started on Saturday at 4:00, the vigil of Advent. And so, we participate with patience and hope. For we know how the story ends.

SUFFERING IS...SUFFERING

Day 12: *God is bringing about a good, and yet I am full of sorrow. I trust Jesus completely. I abandon myself to His Will and yet the pain and sorrow remain. I was looking through Franz's phone to see what obligations of his needed to be taken care of. I found a voice message Franz left to himself where he was practicing his best man speech for his younger brother Bernhard's wedding, which is coming up on January 2. A joyful event that Franz will not be able to attend. We are struck again with such profound grief over a life that was and will no longer be.*

Our faces stained in grief we looked at each other. Why was this so hard? Why can't we overcome this? Why can't we see past the sorrow and rejoice in God? For we have seen the good. We know the good. We want the good. And yet, we cannot stop the vale of tears. We cannot lift the staggering weight of grief. Walter and I sit across the table in the hotel room and just look at each other in confusion. In all our sorrows and tribulations, never have we been so overwhelmed with sorrow. So, we cast our prayers to God, and he shows us:

"And in his anguish, He prayed more earnestly, and His sweat became like drops of blood falling to the ground" (Luke 22).

This is our God. Our infinite, all-knowing God. He knows that He is going to suffer for our salvation. He knows that the absolute greatest good will come from His sorrow. Furthermore, He knows with absolute certainty that the greatest good will come. And still. Still, He is in such anguish that He sweats blood. If our infinite and all-knowing God suffers so greatly, how much more will we suffer? For we do not have His certainty, we only have our faith.

But many ask, if God is infinite, why must we suffer as well? Did He not cover our sins with His blood? St. Paul answers with sobering clarity, *"Now I rejoice in the sufferings for your sake, and in my flesh, I do my share on behalf of his body, which is the Church, in filling up what is lacking in Christ's afflictions"* (Colossians 1:24).

Natural suffering, offered to God in union with Christ's suffering on the cross, brings about actual grace for the Body of Christ. Christ's death and resurrection did not lack anything. The lack is in us silly humans who reject His grace. Who reject the consequences of His cross. By offering up our sufferings for members of the Church, we can help with the salvation of others. Self-sacrifice and suffering in union with Christ's holy cross are the currency of love. It is the greatest act of love we can carry out.

Suddenly the words of St. Gemma, St. Theresa of Calcutta, Padre Pio, and St. Francis are very real to me. I understand that the greatest act of love our Lord can bless me with is to join Him on the cross. To bring me into His plan of salvation.

And though my heart breaks, I take consolation that I am so close to our Lord, Him whom I love. That I have joined Him in the marriage bed of the cross. I take consolation that my dear and loving God, who knows me so well, has given me a suffering that I can bear. I know, in my terrible state of weakness, that nearly anything else would have broken me. But not only has the Great Love prepared me for this moment, He has created me for this moment. He has painted the glorious canvas for this moment.

And so while my husband and I cling to each other in grief, we both know with the clearest certainty that through our very sorrow, an act of mercy is being given to us all.

GOD IS GOOD

God is good. The greatest lesson of them all. The lesson that we need to write upon our hearts. He knows us. He made us. Every DNA, every cell, every fabric of our temperament. He made us and He knows what we can endure. Oh, if I could only shout this message to the world and all the while remember it myself. God is good. And so, just when I thought my heart would never recover. Just when I thought I might die of love and sorrow, God gave me such blessed relief and joy.

Day 13:
They that hope in the LORD will renew their strength,
they will soar as with eagles' wings.
They will run and not grow weary,
walk and not grow faint.

I was in church waiting for Mass to start, when I receive a call from the hospital. Heart pounding, I answer the phone in a husky voice, "Hello?"

"This is Franz's nurse, Ana. Can you hear me?"

I rush out of the church, barreling past old ladies just coming into church, practically knocking them down like bowling pins as I rush for the door. I imagine everything terrible.

I finally make it outside. "Yes!" I practically shout. "This is Christy."

"Can I word vomit on you?"

"Yes, please word vomit on me!" I can barely hear her for the pounding of my heart. Please, God. Please.

"So, Franz is doing great!" I sit down on the ground, almost dizzy.

"Yes, please go on."

"He had a great night. We've taken him off all pain and sleepy drugs. We took him off the lung medicine, and his lungs are absorbing oxygen on their own. He still has a fever and pneumonia. He

is talking away, mouthing words and sentences. He wants to know if his dog had puppies."

I was literally gasping for air, joy so overtaking my body. "Thank you, thank you, I will see him this afternoon."

I spent the day in clouds of happiness, made only happier by the news that Nova indeed had her puppies, eight beautiful puppies!

I waited for 3:00 when visiting hours began and hurried through the halls. Entered the ICU, donned a plastic robe, and rushed in to see if indeed my son was there. He looked at me with bright blue eyes and opened his arms to me. I was overwhelmed with the greatest imaginable joy and rushed into his arms and felt his arms wrap around me. I just breathed in the moment.

I stood back and surveyed him. He just smiled at me. I smiled at him. This. This is Adoration. Then he mouthed "puppies." First things first! I showed him the puppy video and such a smile! I told him about the beautiful Aussie that courted his Nova and he smiled happily. He approved.

Then, he asked about dental school and I told him all the news, that they were willing to do most anything to help him succeed. Another smile. I showed him the beautiful picture his friends had made with them all at school and he took the time to study each picture. Another smile.

Then he asked about his dad. I told him Dad was going crazy, stuck in the hotel, and crying all the time, but he was becoming a saint, so that was good. Smile.

I was making my boy smile and chuckle, and that was what I have been waiting for.

I told him about all the posts, the support and the prayers. Tears came from his eyes, tears of joy and awe. I laughed and stumbled over my words; half-finished sentences barely able to contain my joy. And he just smiled and smiled, loving his mama, soaking it in.

Then, he looked at me most earnestly and mouthed, "Pray for the world." I was taken aback. Not just his town, or his family or friends. But the world. I asked him if that is what he was doing. He nodded gravely. "Pray," he said again urgently. I told him we would.

He asked me, "When can I go home?" My heart skipped and fell: "Soon, Franz, soon. We need to get you out of here, and then you go to rehab, and then you come home. We are going to wheel you up the back steps that you built and through the double French doors you helped with and then we will figure it out." Smile.

Then he asked "Wedding?" Bernhard's wedding. "Can I go?" I looked at the nurse and told her, "Jan. 2 is his brother's wedding, in Mariposa." She said, "Well, you have to get your lungs strong, so you are not on the ventilator. And then you have to get permission because they have to arrange it." No one wants to say the truth. That Franz is still fighting for his life, and he will be lucky to be out of the ICU at all. I am gutted by the sorrow of what he cannot yet see.

After a while, he appeared tired. No doubt I've worn him out. I asked him if he wanted me to read "The Perfect Joy of St. Francis"? He nodded. So, I read him a story about a saint who gave up riches, glory, and fame and chose to follow God in humility. I don't know what he is thinking, but he lay back in peaceful repose. I had such delightful flashbacks from when I read to him as a little boy, stories about saints who were martyrs and heroes.

After a while, my eyes hurt. I ask him if he wants to pray a chaplet. He nods his head and makes the motion of the sign of the cross. Again, I remember when he was a little boy, but his face is that of a man and he is perfectly solemn. I start the chaplet and he grabs my hand and I ask if he wants me to use his fingers to count the prayers. He nods. Again, memories of teaching my boy to pray, as I hold each finger to count the ten prayers. He mouths the prayers and I see tears in his eyes. Again, I wonder in love and awe of what he is thinking.

Nurse announces that tomorrow they are making him sit up, which will help his lungs and try and activate his core. They will move his legs and get his blood and muscles flowing. One giant step forward!

Visiting time is up and I give him another hug and tell him I love him. He looks at me with love and such peaceful happiness.

I walked away this time with such lightness of heart. I practically fly back to Walter to tell him the good news!

RECOVERY

Day 14: *I walked in, and Franz was sparkling-eyed and smiling. I told him stories about all the different paraplegics who have called us and told their stories. We smiled and laughed together.*

He kept asking to work out and the nurses were busy. Nurse told me "We already work him out four times a day and he bugs us all day long to do more." I laugh out loud and say, "I told you he had the heart of a lion!"

We talk and then he asks to say a rosary—he wants joyful today. Then finally the nurses come in for exercise. Everything goes wrong, he knocks the ventilator out of his throat, but he is doing his arm exercises anyway as he is literally gasping for air. They are yelling "Stop Franz!" His blood pressure starts to tank, and he is going white, but nonetheless, he switches to the other hand and is pumping that arm. They are still getting the vent in and trying to lay him down.

They finally get him down and get him taken care of. As soon as he can breathe, he starts scolding them. He is frowning and mouthing a mile a minute. The nurse is trying to figure out what he's saying.

I am laughing out loud and translate: "Look there is an order on how these things go. You have to follow the routine. I can only exercise four times a day so each one matters. You shouldn't have quit!"

The nurse scolds him back: "Look we are here to keep you alive. It doesn't do any good if you pass out!" Franz is shaking his head, disgusted.

I reminded him that he needs to have patience and long suffering. He nods his head meekly. I remind him to offer up his sorrows for the body of Christ and salvation of souls. He nods meekly and grabs my hand. "I'm sorry, I'll do better."

I smile and say, "Badass," and he winks.

It was a great day!

Day 15: *Feast of Our Lady of Guadalupe*
This is a very special feast day. When I walked into Franz's room, I pretty much expected a surprise. And boy! Did I get one!

Franz was in a king-size chair looking pretty dang proud of himself. I have to admit, I wasn't sure what to think or say, except that he looked like a king. Silly Mom. The nurse said to me: "He has been holding out since ten this morning, waiting for his mama to come, so he could show her." I was immediately touched, but still confused.

Finally, I broached the divide of ignorance. "Uhhh...Can you explain the chair to me?" She explained: "This is a total body workout. His body has to keep his blood pressure up, work his lungs, move his blood." She went on, "Most people can only manage this an hour before they lose blood pressure, but your son wanted to stay here until you came so he could show off." Tears in my eyes. For his love. And because I couldn't possibly understand how sitting in a chair could exhaust a person. That was the gulf between him and me.

I smiled at him behind my mask. I ask him, "Is it really a total body workout?" And remember to whom I'm asking this. He nods happily. Yes. And I can see he has that happy, exhausted glow of a man who has physically used all his strength. He is so proud to show me. I am so humbled by his love for his mama.

I have a box full of letters from friends, family, and a box of letters from children. We carefully read each one. A smile, a twinkle in his eye, a look of love for a friend. Many of them are relationships from school that I know nothing about. They all love and admire my son and I am pleased that the boy I raised became a man who has friends who love him.

He tells me that the priest came last night and brought him Communion (the tiniest bit), and he has a bright smile on his face when he tells me. I nod. Beautiful. Then I ask him if he is praying and offering his sufferings to our Lord. He nods solemnly. I am his mother, and the care of his soul is first.

I tell him: "There are many that have asked for prayers. That need help. Can you pray for them?" He nods and motions for me to write them down. I mention some names and situations. He motions again to write them down.

Then he asks to say a rosary. I can see he is sleepy. The nurse lowers the back of the chair into a reclining position. I start the rosary and watch as he makes the sign of the cross. The deliberate effort it takes catches my breath. He mouths to me, "Pray for the world and all those who have asked for prayers." I nod and say out loud our petitions. I ask which mystery and he says the joyful.

We pray the rosary; I notice him trying to move the beads through his fingers. I also notice that he can't tell when the rosary has slipped away. I jump to my feet to put the rosary back into his hands. He wants so much to finger each bead, but this he must work out on his own.

After the rosary, he asks me to read. I pull out The Perfect Joy of St. Francis. We lower the lights and I read on, about the old priest who has honeybees and goats, who recognizes the saint in the eager youth who has come to him. There is such a feeling of peace and tranquility in the room. The nurse comes in and works on Franz. She whispers, "I like hearing your mom read." I look up and Franz smiles and nods. I could not be happier.

We talk about going to rehab and what it will be like. My son has moved from grief to joy to resolve, and I am pleased. In a week, I will go home to mother my other children, to plan for Christmas and a wedding. I tell him I will leave in seven days. He nods. He understands, though I can see the sadness breach the corner of his eyes. I will for him to be strong and courageous.

My time has come to an end. I give him a hug and say goodbye. My heart catches every time. A mother's love is as infinite as God's love, because that is the source. All love shares in His love.

DARK NIGHT OF THE SOUL

Day 17: *The nurse informed me before I enter the ICU that his lungs are doing great, he breathed on his own for three hours. He is healing well from pneumonia*

However, when I went into the room what I saw was a sad boy. I came to him, and he mouthed: "I'm so sad to miss Christmas. All the presents, all of us bundled together on the couch, laughing, and joking. Singing with my family and then playing games afterward outside."

My heart just opened up and fell into pieces. I told him, "I'm so sad I have to leave on the twentieth. I'm so, so sad, but I have to have Christmas for everyone else. We were thinking of having Christmas here, but no one can visit you anyway and we'd all end up FaceTiming you, which we can do from home." He nodded and he understood.

And then he went on, "I'm so used to doing things, to thinking about things, to setting new goals, to talking to people, and I'm just sitting here doing nothing! I can't even hold a book to read!"

I sighed deeply. "I know. I know. But listen, you need to pray, you need to go deep into your spiritual life and listen to what God is telling you. You need to let Him form your heart to His. He needs you to be quiet for this. Take this time to just quiet your soul and listen. He loves you. And apparently He needed to drop you to the ground to get you to listen." Franz smiled sadly and listened. I asked what he wanted to do, and he said, "Just hold my hand." We sat there for a long time, just quiet. I am trying to absorb his sorrow. It is all I can do.

It was time for the nurses to do something for him, so I left the room. I bowed my head and prayed to St. John of the Cross, please, help my son enter into the quiet of his faith, help him to come so close to the Lord, so the rest of the world falls away and it's just him and our Lord."

Right then a nurse comes to me and says: "Franz stopped breathing. He coded." I look at her. What does she mean? "His heart stopped beating," she explains. I rush with her to his room; Franz had his eyes closed and was pale. Nurse immediately assures me, "He is breathing now, but unconscious."

I have no words. I thought we were past this.

She says to me, "He is awake now." I can't go to him because the room is filled with doctors. A doctor comes up to me. I asked him why this happened. He explains: "Well, it happens because of the spinal injury, the body has two systems, and they are having a hard time communicating. It usually happens the first month after the injury." I ask if there was any brain injury. No, they got it quickly, they are prepared. I can't believe this is happening. Just nothing prepared me for this. Not when he was doing so well.

Finally, I am allowed in. I hug him and look at him. He said, "I didn't think I was going to make

*it. But it was better than dying as a martyr, so I
was OK with it." Oh my God. My heart. My heart.
It is barely holding together. I sit next to him and
hold his hand. He asks me to say a rosary. I begin. I
can barely pray the words in between the sobbing.
Franz holds my hand and rubs my arm with the
other hand and makes a comforting sound with
his mouth. "It's OK, Mom. It's OK." I try to swallow
my cries for his sake. I tell him, "You're making me
a saint." He smiles and I smile.*

*I finish the rosary and we sit there for a long
time as he falls asleep. Finally, visiting is over. I
take my hand away, and his eyes flash open, like
the baby you try and leave in the middle of the
night. But it is a man who gazes at me. His eyes
full of love. I smile and say, "You just rest, and don't
do anything stupid while I'm gone!" He nods and I
say, "I love you." He mouths back "I love you, Mom."*

*Back at the hotel, I am sobbing with Walter as
I tell him the story. Both of us are crying and praying. Some days are harder to be a saint than others.*

I thought again about God giving up His son and Abraham who did not have to. God asks us each to love Him above
all else. In this journey toward Christmas, He asks Walter and
me to give up everything for love of Him. For God, in giving
up his Son, has set the example. What a great act of love it
was to let His only Son be crucified for our sins. For the sins
we are not sorry for. For the sins we hide away in the dark
of night. And here I am, not wanting to give up my son for
the God who is all good and all loving. I am humbled by my
humanity and pray for courage. I tell our Lord the hardest

thing a parent can say. "Lord, if you want my son, you can have him, for I love you above all things. I trust you and know that you are good and that all things you work are good." And then I pray that, like Abraham, a lamb will take his place.

WALKING AWAY

My time was drawing to a close. Franz will not be home for Christmas. His heart was breaking. He will not be able to go to his brother Bernhard's wedding. All he wanted during those long days in the ICU was to go to Bernhard and Hannah's wedding. This too he was being denied. I know there is great spiritual growth in his soul. I know with the eyes of faith. But all I could see was a broken man filled with sorrow. I prayed over and over that underneath the brokenness a saint was being formed. It was the only thing that mattered. But oh, how easily those words came to me twenty days ago, "know that this is for your salvation and the salvation of souls." I had no idea how hard they would be to live out. Watching Franz go through these dark nights was the hardest thing I have ever done. I pray for all the mothers and fathers who have watched their children lose their faith, watched them go astray, or stood at their funerals. We are united in a love so strong for our children, that we would die for them if we could. We pray, we pray so much for all those children. We pray for parents. We pray for those who have lost their faith. For it seems so very true that we are all united in the cross of Christ. But the greater truth is that we can also be united in His resurrection, and *that* is the only thing that matters.

I must go home for Christmas and Bernhard's wedding. I have eight other children who have not had their parents for a very long time. I love them as much as I do Franz. It is the hardest thing I have ever done, to leave my suffering son for the sake of the other children.

Franz's lungs have finally grown strong enough to lay flat for surgery. He needs to have a second piece of hardware put in his neck to stabilize it permanently. This spinal cage will be flexible and range about eight inches long, so he will be able to move his neck while keeping it secure. It is a long and dangerous surgery, and so we pray and again offer our son into the hands of God. Trusting that whatever outcome is given to us, we will have the strength to accept.

We finally received the call, at the end of a long, fractured day, that he has come out of surgery and is doing well. We collapsed in relief.

Day 20: *Surgery successful, neck cleared for full motion and rehab. Lungs are healing. Next few days are about pain management.*

As my time winds down with Franz, I become more melancholy and more pensive. Only two days left, and they are destined to be filled with pain. But perhaps that is the role of the mother, made manifest in Our Lady who fell before the cross, wishing to absorb the infinite pain of her son, and would have died, had not angels held her up.

I sat with Franz today, he was worn down and in pain. He tried to be brave, he wanted to look at his new iPad, but his neck was really hurting. I told him, "Please, you just rest. You had a big surgery, you rest, while I read these cards." He laid back but soon had big tears filling his eyes. I got the nurse and told her. She brought his pain medicine. But instead of sleeping, he coughs. This is good for the lungs but hurts his neck and shoulders. More pain. No sleep. The inside of his throat is raw from so much suctioning, but they could give him nothing topical, for it would drain into his lungs.

I could do nothing for him. So, I showed him silly family videos, which made him smile. I read him the many military cards, which made him smile. I read notes that had been sent to me testifying to being renewed in strength, courage, and faith because of Franz, and he listened soberly and with surprise.

I said the rosary with him, and he held the beads, unable to move them through his fingers. He was still in pain but trying to sleep, so I said the Chaplet of Divine Mercy and he appeared calmer. He put his hand out for me to hold it. Finally, I sat there in silence, just holding his hand. Realizing that perhaps this was "mother-ness" in its entirety. Just holding the ones you love and giving comfort.

Finally, he mouthed to me, "At least I'm not blind." I said: "Yes, and at least you have your head! I love your charming, smart, kind, and faith-filled head." He laughed a bit at that and nodded. Count your blessings. Yes, indeed. I held out my hands about twelve inches and said, "At least you have this much" (distance from mid-chest to head) and he laughed a bit more.

I told him it was Thursday, and I would come on Friday and Saturday, but then I would have to go. I explained that after that, it would be his father who would come.

It occurred to me that I was there for the brokenness, when he could not speak, or even cry. He could only look at me with pain-filled eyes. But I was also there to be impressed when he had achieved a new trick. "Look at me, Mom! Look at what I can do!"

But Walter would be there for the building up of a man. By the time Walter would come, the pain from the surgery would have passed, his lungs would be clear, and Franz would be preparing for rehab. Yes, the mother would hold, and the father would build.

I sat there enjoying some of my last time with him.

We sat for a little more. In silence, holding his hand. Then he said, "You should go." He nodded in assurance. And then: "You have been such a support to me. Thank you, Mom." And for no reason at all, I burst out crying and could barely stop. He hugged me and comforted me, and my heart felt as if it had reached the bottomless depths of love.

I told him: "Good night. Be at peace. I will see you tomorrow."

I walked away. Rushing into the waiting arms of my husband, so he could hold me up when I had not the strength.

END OF ADVENT 2020

Day 24: *When I left Franz, he was so sad and frustrated to be stuck in a body that couldn't do anything. I cried with him and tried to encourage him that it would get better, even if we didn't know how much.*

Meanwhile, we have said the St. Andrew novena, which begins like this:

"Hail and blessed be the hour and moment in which the Son of God was born of the most pure Virgin Mary, at midnight, in Bethlehem, in piercing cold."

We have been reflecting on this phrase since the first day of Advent, the morning after Franz's accident. So, when Franz was expressing his anguish at not being able to walk, or even talk. I thought about our God, this "little baby, born alone in the piercing cold." I thought about how God, the infinite, is trapped not only in a finite human, but trapped in the body of a baby, that cannot talk or walk. And suddenly my son was the earthly source of profound reflection on the generosity of God. For though Franz was a man trapped in a body that did not work, how much more frustrating and humbling would it be for God to be trapped in a human body.

183

I told him about this, and as he nodded, I thought that perhaps this reflection was more for me than for him, because I think right now his mental torture is extreme, and I think he just has to make his own journey. He has to become the amazing man that God is giving him the opportunity to be.

Such it was that we left him. With hugs and tears and breaking hearts.

Home we arrived. The house was beautifully decorated for Christmas. There was rejoicing and laughter, and we realized how long it has been that we had lived in our private house of sorrow. We Zoomed with Franz, and when the meeting started, he was upset, the same old Franz who couldn't achieve his goals. We know this Franz well. But we told him about our day, about Christmas lights, and adventures. Puppies were randomly thrust into the camera and Franz, literally despite himself, began to smile. William and Karl got into an argument about which animals can see in the dark and do heat sensors count as seeing. Franz began to smile because he realizes that outside his private purgatory, there are Christmas lights and puppies, brothers arguing important topics, and the silly laughter of sisters. I came to see that in God's perfect timing, it is good that we are home.

That was my song of hope for this Advent. Light from darkness. We know how the story ends. Good always triumphs and don't let anyone tell you any different.

CHAPTER 9

The Greatest Battle

JANUARY 2021

After forty days and forty nights, Franz was cleared to go to Craig Hospital, one of the best in the world. Forty days and forty nights. Used by God to represent a period of testing, preparation, and purification. A time before a transformation. Christ in the desert. Alone and fasting. Moses in the desert. Noah in the ark. All throughout the Bible, the number forty weaves its way through the Old and New Testaments, signifying purification before a great event.

He spent three months at Craig Hospital, most of it recovering from one medical emergency after another. Walter and I spent alternating weeks with him, as only one visitor was allowed, not to mention that we had children at home and work that needed tending to. There were so many three o'clock mornings, driving to the airport, flying, landing in Colorado, and then driving to the hospital, arriving at the end of a long day.

Franz endured so much pain, fear, and loneliness during those three months. At one point he told me: "I am a faithful soldier. I obey because I know my Master is fighting a great battle. He knows where I must stand and what assault I must bear. I don't understand and I don't like it. But He must need suffering to be offered up. We will pray for the world and for my list of petitions."

THE LOST GARDEN

I talked to Franz last night, he said: "So here I am, Mom, hanging out with Jesus on the cross. Letting Him purify me and make me what He wants. I don't like it. I don't understand it. But I obey Him. I am here and I love Him. And He loves me."

And now, I sit before our Lord, my head aching in pain, my body protesting against the hard bench, and my spirit rebelling against my broken heart. What is this rebellion and indignation against pain? It is because deep in my soul is the memory of the lost garden, our lost earthly paradise from which we were condemned to leave. We all want that garden back. We want to run naked in an earthly paradise without suffering or sacrifice. We try to re-create it on earth with immodesty, self-indulgence, drugs, and sin. We are willing to sacrifice whatever it takes to keep that illusion. But the truth is that the remedy against that locked door is joining Christ on the cross. Through His cross, we are given life. Through His stripes, we are healed.

My son's constant state of obedience has struck me to the core. For I realized that I am not such a good soldier as he. No, I cry and scream against the night. I want my son to be healed. I want to make it better. I want to fix him. I want from the depths of my heart for this to all go away. I want that garden back that my mother, the Eve, lost for us all.

I think about her sin and realized it runs deep in my veins. She had everything, perfect joy and happiness, all the fruits of the garden, the just and good love of a man, and the friendship of God himself. Why, why would she forgo all that and eat of the fruit that was forbidden? It is because she thought she knew better. She wanted to know it all. She wanted all the power. For knowledge is power and if you have the map, you don't have to follow the guide. And here I sit, wishing for the map. Wanting to know. Rebelling against the Guide.

If Satan offered me the key to fixing Franz, would I take it? Or would I, like Franz, remain obedient and offer up my broken heart for the salvation of souls? Would I fight the most important battle alongside my son, or would I taste the fruit and walk away as a coward who runs from duty?

I must fight against the generational sin of pride and disobedience in my ancient mother. I must, as Christ, be obedient to the cross. I must pray for humility, for it is only by humility that I can say no to my pride and yes, to He Who Loves. I must sacrifice for those whom God has brought to me, most especially for my husband and children. Sacrifice in the daily death of self in order to feed, clothe, and love those whom God has put in my care. For it is in the small acts of sacrifice, in the small acts of yes to God that we can slowly make our way back to joy. That we can find some portion of happiness and that lost garden.

By now tears of sorrow for what is lost, and tears of joy for what is found, fall freely from my face. I walk with longing toward the confessional, for I realize that I have committed the sin of pride, of thinking I know better than God. I know that my son, in his simple, broken humility, has found a great truth; the incredible importance and necessity of obedience to our Lord, and to our God.

THE WIDOW'S MITE

After three months, the military finally made its way through all the paperwork and called me. "He is our boy, and we want him home." So, they flew Franz from Colorado to Palo Alto, California, to the best VA Medical Center this side of the Rockies. We endured COVID shutdowns that prohibited Franz from seeing visitors. Franz endured five long months of loneliness, rehabilitation, and healing.

And finally. Finally, eight months after the accident, Franz was brought home. He was brought home to a town that had fought alongside him for those eight long months and that rejoiced at his return, lining the streets with signs and happy, joyful waves. What man does not rejoice with his neighbors when a lost sheep returns?

It has been a long and painful journey. But in this time, Walter and I have clung to each other and fought for our family. We have given Christ our suffering and trusted in His miracles. That Franz is with us today, healthy in mind, body, and soul, is a miracle in itself. That so many have walked this journey with us is perhaps the greater miracle.

A young man came up to me the other day. I know him vaguely; he has been in and out of jail and has been working hard on providing honestly for his family. He told me, "Walking with Franz this past year has made all the difference." He continued: "I looked at Franz and thought 'No excuses.' When he had his accident, I quit the drugs and found a job. I have been clean since then. Franz inspired me to do the right thing."

I was overwhelmed by this testimony.

Another friend told me: "I just might come back to the Catholic faith. I was baptized a Catholic, but I left the church a long, long time ago. But Franz inspired me to come home."

These testimonies are the incredible works of faith. What have we done? With God's grace and the prayers of so many, we have managed, like Mary, to say "yes" to God acting in our lives. And He has produced so much goodness and so much grace. We are the two loaves and five fish that were used to miraculously feed the crowd. We are the widow's mite.

***

JANUARY 1, 2022, SOLEMNITY OF MARY

"She treasured all these things and pondered them in her heart."

This past year has been an exquisite year of both pain and joy.

I have rejoiced in the new life, in the wide-open eyes of newborn babies, in the laugh of a toddler, in the adoring gaze of a young mother upon her child. Watched a war-weary husband come home from fighting the evils of the world and turn into a laughing grandpa full of mirth and funny faces.

I have watched my young sons take on the care of their brother, with wit, kindness, and the duty of soldiers. Watched them rise at dawn, before school, to care for him and be the last to bed as they prepare him for sleep. A duty they choose and which they execute with both laughter and gravity.

I have watched my son take on the most difficult challenge of his life and pick himself up over and over as each wave of grief washes over him. Watched him, rise again and again with a determined smile and persevering faith.

I have watched my children circle around their family with a love so deep it makes me gasp. I have been privileged and graced with friends who remained true even though I have been absent. Friends who hold out their hands in friendship, even if I have nothing more to give them. I have been humbled by the prayers of so many friends and strangers that I cannot count them, nor can I ever repay them.

I have been allowed to walk in the footsteps with Mary, as she grieved, almost to the point of death, for her Son. I have kissed the face of Christ on the crucifix and joined my pain to His for the salvation of souls.

All these moments I ponder in my heart and treasure. I do not understand them, but they are, each of them, gifts from the great and beautiful God, and so they are my treasure.

The honor of motherhood is a blessed gift. For, as mothers, we are the first to feel our child's little kicks and scampering in the womb. We are the first to hold the tiny infant and bring it to our breast. We are the first to wipe the tear, to hold the baby clutching us in fear or in grief. We see the first wobbly steps and the hilarious laugh over something so small as a ball bouncing on the floor.

I think of Mary and realize how much I have come to understand about womanhood, in the love a mother has for her child. For even if the child is from the heart instead of the womb, it is the woman's ability for sacrificial love that defines her. I think of the incredible women I have known who, whether they could not have children or their children were grown, have adopted my children and loved and helped them along the way. Their love making the difference.

I think of all the precious moments Mary shared with our Lord. I think of all the moments she pondered and held dear. I think of the searing of her heart as He walked those steps, beaten and bloody, to His death.

Let us also ponder these things in our heart. For the more we contemplate her holy motherhood, the more we know of her Son, our God.

CONCLUSION—A MOMENT IN TIME

Those paintings that I gazed at so long ago, in awe and wonderment, I have been privileged to touch in my own life. I have been blessed with the sacred love between husband and wife. I have weathered the battle for good over evil and seen good triumphant. I have borne some of the sufferings of martyrs and had the privilege of holding my son, like the Madonna, and seeing Christ. Those paintings, once my greatest inspiration, became my companions. And for this, I am honored and privileged. I do not pray for suffering; I do not like suffering. But I pray daily the one prayer that I can make with courage and conviction: "Lord, help me to love you more and more every day."

And so, I have described for you, in my awkward and limited words, my painting. It is a beautiful painting, for it was created by God, the Father Almighty, creator of heaven and earth. Within its frame, it has all the parts of magnificence: A battle. A kiss. Fiery steeds and agrarian pastures. The blood of the crucified and the suffering of martyrs. The laugh of families and the look of lovers. It is a magnificent painting of a battle. The Greatest Battle, the battle for souls. Mine and yours.

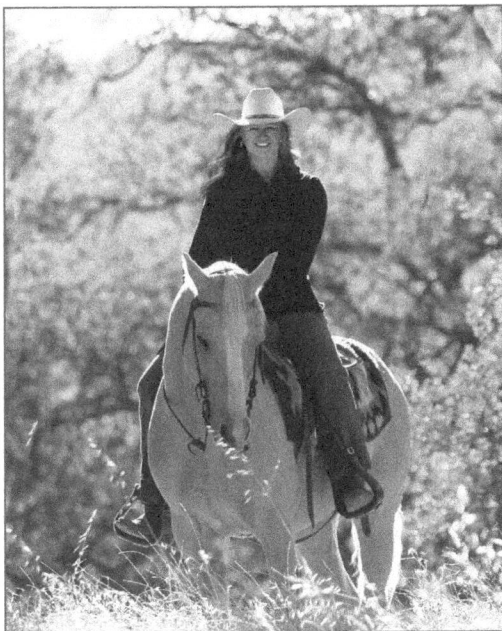

Author photo by Lois Reed

Christy Wall has been writing for both Catholic and public institutions for many years. She currently writes a blog, *Country Spun Gold*, where she delights her readers with tales of country life, children, and humor.

When Christy is not writing, she is taking photographs—both as a professional and a mom. Her favorite subjects are her nine children and many grandchildren on her small ranch. She loves riding the family horses with her children and enjoys nothing more than a wild gallop over the hills near her home.

Christy has been homeschooling for almost thirty years and has worked with multiple programs. She considers daily life on the ranch the best teacher her children have had thus far.

Made in USA - Kendallville, IN
81511_9798886790139
08.26.2022 2027